RAMAYANA

FOR CHILDREN

ARSHIA
SATTAR

RAMAYANA
FOR CHILDREN

Illustrations by Sonali Zohra

juggernaut

JUGGERNAUT BOOKS
KS House, 118 Shahpur Jat, New Delhi 110049, India

First published in hardback by Juggernaut Books 2016
Published in paperback 2019

Designed by Haitenlo Semy

10 9 8 7 6 5 4 3 2 1

ISBN 9789353450434

For sale in the Indian Subcontinent only

Printed and bound at Replika Press Pvt. Ltd.

Contents

Ayodhya

Once, long ago, there lived a king named Dasharatha. He ruled a peaceful and prosperous kingdom bordered by rivers and forests. His capital city, Ayodhya, was rich and splendid. It lay amidst fields of green, its buildings were tall and white, its streets were wide and clean, its people happy and healthy. Everything was as it should be – the rains were gentle and came on time, crops were sown and harvested, food was plentiful and there was neither sickness nor poverty among the people.

Priests performed the sacred rituals, soldiers guarded the land and protected the weak, farmers tilled and sowed. And while cobblers made shoes and goatherds tended their flocks, and jewellers created beautiful ornaments and barbers shaved and cut and styled people's hair, there were also those whose purpose it was to serve other people.

Despite how wonderful everything was in the land, there was a deep sadness in the palace. For though the king had three wives, he had no children. Dasharatha realized that he would have to ask the gods and the sages for help in this matter. He called a council of learned men and he asked if they knew how he could have sons who would continue his line and rule his kingdom wisely and well, as he had done.

The learned men talked among themselves and consulted other learned men. And then, they told Dasharatha that deep in the forests of his kingdom lived a young ascetic named Rishyashringa, 'the Sage with the Horn'. This young man had never lived in human company and had the power to bring rain to thirsty lands. He also had the power to produce sons for childless kings because of the terrific austerities he had performed with such devotion and concentration.

Dasharatha sent for the Sage with the Horn and asked him to perform the special ritual which would produce male heirs for his kingdom. Rishyashringa did as the king asked and a grand ceremony was performed around a sacred fire with the king and his queens in attendance.

As the ritual was coming to an end, an enormous creature, red in colour and dressed in crimson garments, arose from the flames. He held a bowl in his hands and he presented it to King Dasharatha. In a voice that roared and crackled like the fire itself, he told Dasharatha to distribute what was in the bowl among his queens. Dasharatha bowed his head and joined his palms in gratitude and respect as he accepted the gift from the fiery being. And then he shared the sweet, milky substance that was inside the bowl among his wives – Kaushalya, Sumitra and Kaikeyi.

Soon, the sadness in the palace turned to rejoicing. All three queens were pregnant. Under bright stars that promised fame and good fortune, Kaushalya was the first to give birth. Her son Rama was born with a face like the moon and marked with all the lucky signs that confirmed that he would grow up to be a great king. Soon after that, Kaikeyi gave birth to Bharata and then Sumitra gave birth to the twins Lakshmana and Shatrughna.

Banners and buntings flew from the tops of Ayodhya's white buildings as the people celebrated the birth of their princes. The streets were strewn with flowers as the citizens clapped and sang and danced, and shared food and drink with each other, turning the city into a great big happy party. Dasharatha wept tears of joy as he gazed lovingly at his sons and he thanked the gods for their attention to his prayers. He distributed gifts among all his people – cows and clothes and jewels and food, and toys for all the children. With the birth of the boys, Ayodhya's future was finally secure.

The princes grew up together, laughing and tumbling and playing in an atmosphere filled with love and friendship. Rama, the eldest, was always the leader. He was easily the best at everything – his arrows flew straighter, he leapt higher and ran faster, he learned the sacred texts before anyone else did and when they discussed the complex arts of kingship Rama was just and gentle, wise and practical.

Everyone knew that he would be the next king, not only because he was the most suited to the job but also because Dasharatha loved him the best. The three queens watched over their sons with equal delight and pleasure, sharing the joys and cares of motherhood as the boys with scraped knees and dirt-streaked faces grew into handsome young men who wielded their bows and arrows with as much ease as they debated law and politics with their teachers.

One day, when all was quiet and calm, the great sage Vishwamitra arrived at the gates of Dasharatha's palace. Vishwamitra was well known and greatly respected but he was also feared because everyone knew that he would never take no for an answer, not even from the gods. The king rose to meet him and washed his feet with blessed water and gave him the best seat in the court. 'What can I do for you, great sage?' said the king humbly. 'It is my duty to fulfil any wish that you might have.'

'Good,' replied the sage. 'Let me get straight to the point. I have come here to take Rama with me to fight the vicious yakshini Tataka. She has been interrupting my rituals along with her wretched sons. I cannot curse them, for if I display anger by losing my temper, all that I have gained through my austerities will be lost. Prepare Rama to leave with me immediately!'

'But . . . but,' stammered the king, who was very agitated. 'Rama is still a boy. He has not been tested in the arts of combat. Tataka has magical powers – she can fly through the air and tunnel through the earth and swim through water. She can even make herself invisible. You cannot expect my young son to take her on!'

'Very well,' said Vishwamitra, as he rose to go. 'I thought nothing I asked for would be refused in the court of the great Dasharatha. I was wrong, you are like every other king, after all.'

Dasharatha was even more upset. 'Please, sir,' he begged, 'let me come with you. I will kill Tataka. I will send my eight-divisioned army with you, they are a mighty fighting force and have never been defeated. Please don't take Rama.'

'I want Rama for this task. No one and nothing else will do,' said Vishwamitra firmly.

Rama stepped forward and said calmly, 'Let me go, father. I will help the sage. I am ready to fight. And I will take Lakshmana with me.' He turned to the sage and said, 'I shall follow wherever you lead.'

A small smile broke through Vishwamitra's stern expression when he heard Rama's determined words. He left the grand palace with Rama and Lakshmana, who were carrying their gold-tipped bows and their quivers full of arrows fletched with the feathers of sky-soaring eagles. They left the bustling city and travelled through the deep, quiet forests that surrounded it until they came to a vast wasteland. It was dotted with scrubby trees and dried-up ponds. Birds of prey wheeled in the air and a harsh, hot wind blew around them.

Soon, they reached an outcrop of rock that cast a dark and brooding shadow over the earth. 'Come,' said the sage. 'This is where I am performing a ritual that will make me even more powerful than I am now. As soon as I begin, Tataka will arrive with her sons, Subahu and Maricha, and they will harass me and disturb my concentration.

You must kill all three of them. Be alert, for they are mighty and brave. And they can fight in the sky as well as on earth. You have my blessings.'

As the sage settled down to his practice, a great whirlwind arose, scattering dust into the princes' eyes and stinging their faces. 'Lakshmana, it's her!' yelled Rama as he strung his bow. As the wind howled around them, they could see the gigantic Tataka in its midst – sharp-fanged, copper-haired, arms and legs waving, she flew towards them. Her sons followed behind her, equally large and equally frightening. A single blow from Rama sent Subahu and Maricha reeling backwards, so far and so fast that they landed with a splash in the ocean which was thousands of miles away.

Enraged, Tataka charged towards Rama. 'Kill her!' shouted the sage. Lakshmana prepared to loose an arrow that would annihilate the yakshini, but Rama was quicker and sent forth a shower of arrows that pinned Tataka to the ground. 'I can't kill her, Lakshmana,' he said as he slung his bow over his shoulder. 'She's a woman. But I have destroyed her power to move.'

Vishwamitra was pleased with the courage and skills that the boys had shown. 'Rest now,' he said as he patted their backs. 'Tomorrow you shall receive your reward. I will teach you the secrets of the most powerful weapons in the world. They shall make you invincible in battle.'

The next morning, Vishwamitra began his lessons. He taught the princes how to concentrate, how to centre their energies and how to focus their minds and remain calm when they were under attack. As Rama and Lakshmana improved by the day, he showed them how to control their breathing. Finally, he whispered the great secrets to them – magic words that would power and direct the weapons of the gods. He gave Rama mantras for the Vayavya, the Agneya and the Varuneya especially, preparing him to fight and defeat the deadliest enemies.

Then the sage turned the boys away from Ayodhya and led them in an easterly direction. 'I want to take you to Mithila where King Janaka rules,' he said mysteriously. 'He is a king but he has the mind and the wisdom of a sage. His kingdom, Videha, is not as rich as your kingdom of Kosala and his city doesn't have the wealth and splendour of Ayodhya. It is a simple place and its people live off the land. I have heard that King Janaka himself used to plough fields and till the land. His daughters have reached the age when they should be married, but he has set a task for the man who will marry the eldest, Sita.' Lakshmana understood what the sage was hinting at and he winked at Rama, who looked away with a smile.

Vishwamitra entered Mithila, the two princes following behind him, and made straight for the royal enclosure. Although it was small and quite rustic, it was brightly decorated with flowers and leaves and other produce from the fields, and patterns were drawn with rice flour on the ground. Music wafted through the air – they could hear the gentle notes of a flute and the strains of a stringed instrument. Perhaps people were singing as well, for the sound of human voices rose and fell as they drew closer to the central square. The square was crowded and though Rama thought he recognized the king, a distinguished-looking man with a long beard, there was no sign of any princesses.

In the middle of the square was a massive bow, the largest that Rama had ever seen. It was polished to a silvery sheen, like the full moon. Its tips were as bright as the sun and its string, which hung loosely, seemed to hum with energy. It had been dragged into the square by five hundred men pulling an iron cart with eight wheels. Janaka approached the sage and touched his feet, welcoming the princes with a warm smile. 'What can I do for you, my lord?' he asked.

'This is Prince Rama of Ayodhya, son of the mighty monarch Dasharatha. And this is his brother Lakshmana. I want Rama to win the hand of your daughter Sita by lifting the bow,' said Vishwamitra.

Janaka turned his gaze on to the young men, who stood tall and proud, a few steps behind the sage. 'You're welcome to try, Prince Rama. This is Shiva's bow. It has been worshipped by my family for generations. No one has been able to lift it, let alone string it. I should also tell you that my daughter Sita is no ordinary woman. She was given to me by the Earth herself when I was ploughing a field many years ago. Whoever wins her hand must treat her exceptionally well because she is special. Will you promise to do that?'

'I promise to do that,' said Rama simply, looking the king in the eye.

Without any fuss, Rama walked over to the bow. He closed his eyes and made his mind as still and steady as the earth from which Sita was born. He placed his hand firmly on the bridge of the bow. In a trice, he had lifted the bow and with a movement as quick as lightning strung it as well. Before anyone could move, there was a sound like a thunderclap. Rama had snapped the great bow into two pieces. The people of Mithila shouted and stamped their feet in celebration. Rama glanced up at the gallery and was sure that he saw a sweet, bright face vanish quickly behind the reed curtain. He smiled to himself and turned to honour the king.

Janaka was delighted by Rama's extraordinary feat and understood immediately that the man who was going to marry his daughter was as special as she was. 'Come, my son,' he said, putting his arm around Rama's shoulder. 'Let us invite your father and his queens and his entire court to the wedding of all my four daughters with all his four sons. You have won Sita for yourself but I bestow her three younger sisters in marriage on your noble brothers. This happy day will be remembered in Mithila forever!'

The multiple weddings lit up Mithila for days and nights but finally it was time for the young princesses to leave their home and go with their husbands to Ayodhya, a city very different and very far away from their own.

Now that Rama was married, King Dasharatha, who was growing old, thought constantly about the future. He felt that it was time for Rama to ascend the throne of Ayodhya and rule the prosperous kingdom of his forefathers. Rama was accomplished in all the arts of kingship, he was a skilled and courageous warrior, he was loved by his family and his people – there was no reason to delay his coronation. Dasharatha called together his entire court – his ministers and advisers and his generals – as well as kings from neighbouring lands.

In his packed court, he announced in a voice that was as deep as thunder, 'The time has come for me to retire. I have served my people well; I have ruled this earth wisely. My kingdom is prosperous and at peace. I have no enemies and my sons have grown into fine young men. Tomorrow, under the auspicious constellation of Pushya, I shall crown Rama, my beloved eldest son, king of Kosala, ruler of Ayodhya! May you serve him with the same love and loyalty that you have served me.' The kings and ministers and generals gathered there broke into applause. 'Rama! Rama! Hail King Rama! Hail King Dasharatha! Victory to Rama!' they shouted.

The king returned to his private chambers and, all over Ayodhya, the people began to prepare for Rama's coronation. The priests set about collecting all the materials they would need for the ceremony – sandalwood and ghee and flowers, and water that had been blessed. Men and women washed their homes and sprinkled the streets with perfumed water to keep the dust down. Merchants spread out their best wares, young men climbed to the tops of buildings and hung them with banners, young women pulled out their finest clothes and jewels, actors and dancers tried out new performances, musicians tuned their instruments, and even children did their bit by stringing garlands of multicoloured flowers.

In the palace, too, servants ran around getting things ready for the big day. Clothes were perfumed with fragrant oils and scents. Pillars were wrapped in flowers. Oil lamps were lit in the windows and all the corners of all the rooms. Couches were covered in shimmering silks and shining satins, and sumptuous food and drink were laid out on banquet tables in dishes of gold and glasses of silver. There was song and laughter everywhere – not a single pair of hands was idle.

As the servants laughed and talked, word spread about Rama's coronation into the inner apartments. Manthara, who was Queen Kaikeyi's maid, watched the preparations with a heavy heart. Manthara was a hunchback and she had come with the queen to Ayodhya when she got married. She was fiercely loyal to her mistress as she was to Bharata, Kaikeyi's son. Finally, she could bear it no longer and waddled over to where Kaikeyi was getting dressed for the evening celebrations. 'Are you happy at this news? Look at you, you're a fool! What are you doing laughing and smiling and getting dressed in all your finery? As if it was your son who was being crowned king tomorrow!' she snarled.

'O Manthara! Are you in one of your moods? Of course I'm celebrating. Rama is my son, too. He loves me as much as he does his own mother. I am so happy for him. Aren't you?' Kaikeyi smiled as she reached out her hand to the old hunchback.

'Kaikeyi! Be sensible!' screamed Manthara. 'You have no idea what lies in store for you if Rama becomes king. Don't you think it's odd that Dasharatha arranged this coronation while Bharata is visiting his grandfather? What are you thinking? When Rama is king, Kaushalya will be the most powerful woman in the palace. It will make no difference that you are Dasharatha's favourite – Rama will be king. You and your son will be shoved aside, you will have no power, you will have to beg for favours. Is that the life you want to live?'

Kaikeyi was stunned. She pushed away the maid who was weaving flowers into her hair and ordered her to leave the room. She turned to look at Manthara, her eyes wide with horror. 'What did you say?' she whispered. 'Do you think Rama will treat me differently once he is king? Will the old king have no more powers? Will my son have to serve his brother? Will I be a nobody?'

'That is exactly what will happen, Kaikeyi,' said Manthara more calmly. 'Your father did not marry you to an old man so that you could be treated like an old and unimportant woman. He wanted you to be powerful, the favourite wife of a doting husband who would do anything that you asked.'

'O what will happen to me now?' wailed Kaikeyi, tears streaming down her lovely face. 'I don't want to be ignored, I don't want my son to be a servant! What shall I do, Manthara? Help me!'

Manthara sidled over and stood by the queen, stroking her hair and wiping her tears with her hand. 'Listen to me, my dear,' she said. 'All is not lost. We still have a few tricks up our sleeve. We have to make sure that Rama is not crowned tomorrow.'

'But how can we do that? All the preparations have started. The priests have begun the rituals, Rama must be taking his purifying bath as we speak.'

'You must act at once, Kaikeyi,' said Manthara, her little eyes above her pinched nose shining as she spoke. 'You have the ultimate power over Dasharatha. He has promised you two boons that you can ask for whenever you like – ask for them now! Use one boon to banish Rama into the forest for fourteen years, use the other to make your son Bharata king. Come, now. Wipe off your make-up, tear your clothes, loosen your hair. Go to the Anger Room and lie on the floor. Call Dasharatha to you and tell him that you will never speak to him again unless he surrenders to your wishes.'

Kaikeyi did as Manthara had said and threw herself on the floor of the Anger Room, her fine clothes and beautiful hair in a mess. She tore off her necklace and its pearls scattered across the dark floor like stars in the midnight sky. Her eyes were red with angry tears and she commanded her maid, 'Tell the king I want to see him. Now!'

King Dasharatha loved Kaikeyi deeply – she was his favourite queen. He could not bear her unhappiness, or even her discomfort. As soon as he heard that she was in the Anger Room his heart thudded against his ribs and he ran, puffing and gasping, to where she was. He saw her sprawled on the cold floor, wailing and tearing her hair, beating her breast as if the person she loved most in the entire world had died.

'Kaikeyi, Kaikeyi, what is the matter? Why are you in this state? How can I make you happy again?' cried the king as he tried to take her in his arms. She pushed the old king away and shouted, 'Make my son Bharata king and send Rama into the forest for fourteen years! That will make me happy for all time.'

Dasharatha could not believe his ears. Tears rolled down his face as he begged Kaikeyi to change her mind. The mighty monarch, that great king, knelt at her feet, his head bowed, the proud crown of his forefathers touching the floor. 'I did not hear you correctly, my beloved. Surely you did not ask me to send my precious Rama into the forest for fourteen years? He is to be crowned king tomorrow, the preparations have begun. Bharata is his younger brother, he cannot be king. Tell me, what is it that you really want? I will die without Rama!' cried the king.

'You heard me, Dasharatha,' said Kaikeyi, moving her feet away from his grasp. 'Rama to the forest and Bharata on the throne! You gave me two boons when I saved your life in battle when I was a young girl. I did not want those boons then, I had everything I wanted. But I will redeem those boons now. Will you tell Rama or shall I?'

Even as the old king begged and pleaded, Kaikeyi asked for Rama to be brought into her presence. Before long, Rama entered the Anger Room, looking as calm as the moon reflected in still waters. He saw his weeping father lying on the floor and Queen Kaikeyi standing triumphant, her eyes flashing. He bowed to them both and said, 'Mother, you summoned me. Tell me, what is your command?'

'Your father wants Bharata to be crowned king of Ayodhya. And he wants you to live in the forest for fourteen years. Starting tomorrow,' said Kaikeyi, her voice trembling slightly at the awful words she was saying.

'Very well, mother,' said Rama calmly, as he turned to look at his aged father. Dasharatha lay on the floor, his face wet with tears. Rama wiped Dasharatha's tears and helped his father to a seat, murmuring words of comfort and strength. 'Don't worry, beloved sir. Fourteen years will pass in a flash and I'll be back to play chess with you. And let you win,' he smiled gently. Dasharatha let out a howl of anguish and fell into a faint.

Rama bowed to Kaikeyi and said, 'I will make preparations to leave the city in the morning. But I ask a favour of you. Look after my father. Make sure he stays well and happy, do not let him experience any more sorrow than this separation from me. I trust you, mother Kaikeyi. And now, please excuse me. I must share this news with my mother Kaushalya and with my dearest Sita.'

Rama's heart was heavy as he walked through the palace that was being festooned and adorned and polished and swept and perfumed. He knew his mother would be distraught at the sudden turn of events but his concern was for Sita, his gentle wife, whose sadness he would not be able to bear.

As he approached his mother's apartments, he made sure his step was resolute and his face was open and clear. Kaushalya was delighted to see Rama at this unexpected hour. She kissed his forehead and made him sit beside her. 'What are you doing here, my son? You should be meditating and preparing yourself for the rituals of the morning. These coronation ceremonies can be long and very tiring. Here, have some of this honeyed water and eat a few almonds. They'll give you strength of mind,' she said.

'Mother, I will not be crowned tomorrow morning,' said Rama gently. 'My father wishes me to go to the forest and live there for fourteen years. I have come to seek your blessings and say goodbye.'

'O Rama, how you joke', said Kaushalya, laughing. 'You must be nervous about tomorrow. Come, have some almonds. I sliced them myself and they've been soaked in rose water.'

'Mother, it's true,' said Rama softly.

Kaushalya stared at her son, aghast. His face was unclouded, his eyes were bright, his brow was clear. Kaushalya turned pale, as if all the blood in her body had drained away. She knew this was no joke, nor was it a lie. She whispered, 'What happened? Who did this to you? To me?'

'I have just come from mother Kaikeyi's chambers. She told me that our father wishes his son Bharata to be king and that he wishes me to live in the forest,' said Rama. 'I shall live there as an ascetic, eating roots and fruits, thinking about how to make the world a better place, about how to be a better person myself. Mother, I would never have this chance in the palace, even less so as king. Destiny has intervened, it must be the right thing for me to go to the forest.'

Kaushalya's voice was hoarse. 'I waited so long for this moment – the moment my son would be king. I suffered slights and insults for years because your father did not love me enough. But I held my peace because I knew that you were the eldest, that one day you would rule and I would be respected and honoured as your mother, the mother of the king. I can't imagine what deeds I might have committed in my previous lives to have this last chance at happiness snatched away from me like this.' Kaushalya started to wail. She tore her hair and beat her breast.

'Mother, it is my dharma, my duty, to obey my father's wishes,' said Rama.

'And what about your duty to me? Does a son have no obligations to his mother, no dharma that keeps her happy and fulfilled? You should be king, Rama,' she said, bitterly. 'You have already understood that your destiny takes you away from me and from your family.'

Rama sighed as he tried to console his mother. But his mind was already elsewhere. He had to tell Lakshmana, his brother who was like his shadow, his other self. And then there was Sita. What could he say to her that would make any sense at all?

Lakshmana had been standing on the palace terrace, watching the city prepare for Rama's coronation. His heart overflowed with joy, for he knew his brother would be the best king that Kosala had ever seen, better even than their father. He noticed Rama going into Kaushalya's rooms and ran down the stairs to the courtyard, eager for a quiet moment with Rama. He asked the doorkeeper to announce his presence and waited to be invited into Kaushalya's anteroom. Rama came to greet him. He embraced him and led him forward. Expecting to see jubilation and joy, Lakshmana was taken aback at the silence in the room. 'What has happened?' he asked, searching Rama's face for an answer.

'Tomorrow I leave for the forest. Our father wishes me to live there for fourteen years. Our brother Bharata shall be king of Kosala instead of me,' Rama said, his hand on his brother's arm.

'What?' stuttered Lakshmana. 'Our father has exiled you into the forest? That cannot be! He loves you, he trusts you. We love you, we all want you to be king. Our people are already celebrating. How can our father go against the wishes of the people? What about all the preparations for tomorrow?' Unable to think any further, Lakshmana collapsed on to a couch, his head in his hands.

But in a moment, he rose and spoke again. 'Kaikeyi is behind this, I know. I will not let this happen, Rama. This is unjust, it is foolish. We must save the king's honour. He will be a laughing stock when people hear that he succumbed to the wishes of his wife and surrendered his duties as a king. And as a father. This cannot be! Where's my sword? I'll put an end to this business right now!'

'Lakshmana, my brother, I have made up my mind. I will honour my father's wishes because my dharma as a son tells me that this is what I should do. I am going to the forest. Tomorrow.'

Lakshmana set his jaw, as he always did when he had made up his mind. 'Very well,' he said, 'I'm coming with you.' He turned to Kaushalya. 'Mother, you have nothing to fear. I will protect your son and he will come back to you, as he is now, in fourteen years.'

More than ever, Rama felt the need to see Sita, to be in her quiet, steady presence, away from the charged emotions of his mother and brother. He excused himself and went to his own palace, beautiful as a lustrous jewel set in the midst of Dasharatha's royal compound. He entered his chambers to find Sita busy laying out his ceremonial clothes for the morning – the silken garments white as a swan's wing, the soft shawl made from the downy underfur of the mountain goat, the slippers studded discreetly with gems.

He could not help but smile at the pleasure she took in his wardrobe, making sure every day that he looked every inch the prince of men that he was. Often, she called him her 'tiger among men', for he was fearless and majestic, and she had seen how his skin turned gold in the rising sun as he performed the morning worship.

'Sita,' he said, taking her by the hand, 'I have no use for these fine garments. Tomorrow, I will go to the forest for fourteen years. My father wishes it so. I shall wear clothes made from the bark of trees and live as an ascetic.' He saw the flicker of doubt in her eyes and spoke further. 'Bharata, our brother, will be king in my place. Lakshmana will come with me. And you, piece of my heart, my beloved, you shall stay here in the palace with my mother. I shall return to you and love you then as I do now.'

'You shall go to the forest and I shall stay here? What did I marry you for, Rama, if not to share your life, whether it be in the palace as a queen or in the forest as an ascetic,' Sita said, her voice calm and steady. 'I cannot be without you. I shall go where you go.' She looked directly at her husband's face, but Rama could see that her hands shook as she folded away the royal garments.

'Sita, my dear, you have no idea of what the forest is like. You cannot possibly come with me. It is not a place for a woman – there are wild animals and strange creatures the likes of which we have never seen before. There are thorny bushes, the paths are strewn with stones. I shall sleep on a bed of leaves and bathe in cold, rushing rivers. The forest is not a place for you, my darling princess. You are used to silks and soft beds and sweet perfumes.'

Sita's voice rose a little. 'What use are silks and soft beds and sweet perfumes to me if you are not there? What of the wild animals and strange creatures – you are there to keep me safe. What of thorny bushes and stony paths and rushing rivers? They will be nothing to me if I am with you. This palace without you will be full of thorns and stones. I am coming with you, Rama. If Lakshmana can be your companion, so can I.'

Rama knew that there was no point in arguing with his wife, for under her gentle appearance was a will of tempered steel. He remembered that she, born of the Earth, was more familiar with plants and trees and animals than he would ever be. 'Come, then,' he said. 'Be my companion in my exile.'

The day, which should have been a bright day of celebration, dawned cloudy, as if even the sun could not bear to watch Rama's departure from the city. Word of the king's decree had spread through Ayodhya. The citizens stood around in groups, trying to understand what had happened. The flowers in the ceremonial enclosure seemed to wilt, the cheerful banners and buntings on rooftops drooped and sagged. Even the children dragged their feet and erased the colourful decorations in front of their homes.

The palace was shrouded in gloom, its bright towers dull, its vast halls silent. Only Kaikeyi was cheerful, urging Dasharatha to the arched gates where Rama would come to take his leave. 'Don't you want to say goodbye to your beloved Rama? Come now, walk a little faster. It is the auspicious hour, they're about to leave the city.' She laughed as she tried to lead the king to where Rama waited for him. Dasharatha stumbled forward with his arms outstretched, as if he were blind. He held Rama close, tears pouring from his eyes on to Rama's strong shoulders. Sita and Lakshmana bowed to him and to their mothers, asking for blessings that would keep them safe on their journey ahead.

Rama climbed into the royal chariot with his brother and his wife, steadfast and determined. 'Take us to the border of the kingdom,' he commanded, as if he were indeed the king of Kosala.

The people of Ayodhya ran behind the chariot, begging Rama not to leave. They tripped and fell, they were covered in the dust that the chariot wheels raised, they wailed and cried. But Rama gazed straight ahead, his eyes fixed on the destiny that was taking him along an unknown path.

As the chariot sped into the distance and could no longer be seen, Dasharatha collapsed. He pushed Kaikeyi away and called for Kaushalya, pleading with her to take him home. 'Forgive me, Kaushalya,' wept the old king. 'Forgive me!' Before the sun set on that sad day, Dasharatha, his heart broken, died in Kaushalya's arms.

Messengers who rode horses that were as swift as the wind were sent to fetch Bharata and Shatrughna from the kingdom of Kekaya. Knowing that something was terribly wrong, the brothers travelled day and night, barely stopping to eat or rest.

When they saw Ayodhya's towers dull under the morning sun, they feared the worst. Kaikeyi greeted them at the entrance to her chambers. She was full of smiles despite her white clothes of mourning. 'Bharata, my son, you shall be king of Kosala! Your father has died and Rama has been exiled to the forest,' she said, embracing Bharata.

Bharata stumbled backwards, his face aflame. 'What did you say? The king is no more? Rama has left the city? I am to be king? Mother, you must be mad with grief!

'Get away from me, you vile woman,' he spat. 'You have killed the old king and sent the best man in the world into the forest. You shall never be forgiven. I must make amends – I am not the son of a woman who destroyed this family's honour!'

Shatrughna close on his heels, Bharata hurried to where the king's body lay and paid homage. And then, they were taken away to prepare for the funeral rites. Later, they collected his ashes and immersed them in the river Sarayu that bordered their city.

'Where is Rama?' Bharata asked Vasishtha, the royal priest. 'I must make him believe that I had nothing to do with this. I will bring him back to rule the kingdom that belongs to him. Come with me, Shatrughna, you are my only ally. I can only imagine what Rama and Lakshmana think of me.'

The Forest

Rama, Sita and Lakshmana rode in their chariot to the very edge of Kosala. It was evening when they reached the river Tamasa but news of their arrival had preceded them. Guha, the king of the Nishadas, was waiting. He offered them fruit and water and a cushion of leaves under a nyagrodha tree so that they could refresh themselves. Rama dismissed the chariot, bidding an affectionate farewell to Sumantra, the charioteer who had known him since he was a child.

Sita was exhausted, but she put on a brave face as she prepared for her first night outside the city. She recalled that she knew the Earth, that Earth was her mother and would protect her in the days to come.

The Earth would provide her with food and with a warm bed, even with flowers for her hair. A little distance away, Rama and Lakshmana sat with Guha, talking quietly.

'I must dress in clothes of bark,' said Rama. 'Help me, Guha. Show me how to matt my hair, for I must live as an ascetic for fourteen years. Tell me about the roots and shoots that we can eat, show me the berries that will slake our thirst. I have much to learn from you.'

'I, too, shall live as an ascetic,' said Lakshmana. 'Our royal finery is not much use here, is it?' He smiled ruefully as he loosened his quiver. 'But ascetic or not, I'm going to keep my weapons and I'm going to keep them in good order. Rama, you are a warrior, I cannot imagine you without your bow and arrows!'

Rama looked at his brother and his heart swelled with pride and gratitude. He suddenly sensed how much he would need Lakshmana's courage as they faced unknown dangers. He was glad that he was not alone. 'We must leave this kind land and these good people tomorrow,' he said. 'We are still too close to Ayodhya and I promised that I would live in the forest. Guha will set us on our way. We shall have to walk. I wonder how Sita will manage.'

'She will walk between us,' said Lakshmana. 'You will walk ahead and I will bring up the rear. We are both armed. We can face anything. Watch me build a hut for you tomorrow. You'll be surprised!' he went on, feeling a sense of adventure rather than dread.

In the morning, the princes went down to the river to worship the sun, bathe and perform the morning rituals. It was a clear day. A soft breeze blew and carried the fragrance of unfamiliar wild flowers to Sita as she awoke from a dreamless sleep. Since they carried little with them, it was an easy departure. Guha, who had been a good friend of Dasharatha's, accompanied them for a distance and set them on the path to where the sages had their settlements.

For Sita's sake, Rama knew that their journey into the distant forest must be slow and in stages. So he was pleased to spend some time with the sages and their wives, all of whom treated gentle Sita as if she were their daughter. They gave her new clothes and washed her hair

and rubbed her feet with herbal oils. They taught her how to use what the Earth offered so generously. Despite his wife's delight at being with the sages' wives, Rama knew that they had to keep moving.

'Go to the region of Chitrakuta,' said the sage Bharadhvaja. 'It is a pleasant place, with waterfalls and streams and sloping meadows. The rain is gentle and the trees and rocks give you shelter from the sun. Birds and animals live there because it is abundant in food and water. Sita will be comfortable and you and your brother will be at ease.'

Rama, Lakshmana and Sita thanked the sages for their kindness and generosity. They set off, going further, further from Ayodhya, from the palace and their families and their kingdom. They walked easily, stopping to eat and rest by murmuring streams and in whistling groves of fruit-laden trees. Sita pointed out flowers and creepers and birds along the path to her husband, but it was Lakshmana who held them back when he saw a snake sunning itself on the rocks by the side of the path. At night, they slept, warm in their beds of leaves and dried moss in the shelter of trees with wide canopies, watching the stars and listening to the night birds. Sometimes, it was possible to forget that they were in exile, banished from the people they loved. And that fourteen long years away from home stretched ahead of them.

Meanwhile, in Ayodhya, gloom prevailed. Clouds hung over the once bright and happy city. People were still mourning the old king and they fretted about their beloved Rama. They worried about his well-being but consoled each other that Lakshmana was with him and that he would surely protect Rama and Sita from any dangers.

Bharata was sunk in despair, confused and unhappy. He rejected the cloying company of his mother and her scheming maid Manthara. He missed his brothers desperately and he was tormented by the thought that he had to make up for his mother's actions. He certainly did not want to be king and rule Ayodhya.

Early one morning, he roused Shatrughna from his bed and said excitedly, 'Brother, I know what I must do. I will go to wherever Rama is and beg him to take back the kingdom. He must return to Ayodhya and be king of Kosala – we all know that's what our father truly wanted. Come, we'll find Rama and bring him back in a royal procession!'

'Have you asked our advisers and ministers about this?' asked Shatrughna cautiously.

'Not yet. Let them come with us when we go to bring Rama back. I don't want to delay this with meetings and councils and assemblies. Besides, if Rama decides to argue with us, they will be there to persuade him that the only right thing for him to do is return with us,' said Bharata who was almost in the next chamber in his hurry to leave. 'We'll take our mothers as well, so that Rama is convinced that we all want him back, even Kaikeyi. Hurry with your royal garments and weapons! Remember, we're going to bring back our king.'

As quickly as he could, Bharata summoned the members of the royal court and told them to prepare for the journey into the forest.

He alerted the queens' attendants and urged them to make sure that the royal ladies would be comfortable as they travelled. In a few hours, the huge court of Ayodhya was ready to move. Horses, elephants, chariots, priests, ministers, advisers, servants, bags and baggage and ordinary citizens with their children – all followed Bharata and Shatrughna as they rode out of the city on their tawny horses who tossed their manes and jingled their harness bells sweetly as they trotted along.

For all that his heart was filled with joy, Bharata also carried a sadness with him for he knew he would have to tell Rama about their father's death. The princes rode ahead to find out from Guha where Rama had gone. The next day, they led the entire entourage to Chitrakuta.

In the quiet forest, Lakshmana was as alert as ever. As he chopped firewood, he heard a sound like thunder rumbling in the distance. He looked up to see if rain was approaching, but all he saw was a clear, cloudless blue sky. He heard animals moving in the underbrush and he noticed that the bird calls had changed. Something new had entered the forest, something that was alarming and perhaps dangerous. He climbed to the top of the tallest tree he could see and looked out over the forest which now seemed to be heaving and swaying.

'Rama, Rama!' he shouted. 'Bharata has come to Chitrakuta with a huge army. Tell Sita to hide inside the hut and get your bow and arrows ready. He has come here to attack us, I am sure of that!'

'Come down, Lakshmana,' shouted back Rama. 'Bharata would never attack us, he is our brother. There is no need for weapons. We must greet him calmly, with affection. Instead of picking up your bow, prepare the welcome rituals.'

Lakshmana was not so easily convinced and kept his weapons at hand as he stood behind Rama and Sita while they waited for Bharata to reach them. As soon as Bharata saw Rama, he leapt off his horse and rushed to him, tears coursing down his face. Rama held him close in a warm embrace and wiped his tears.

'Rama, I am so sorry for all that has happened. You must know that I had nothing to do with my mother's plans. Come back with me. Take your place as king of our lands and our people,' wept Bharata.

Rama made him sit down and turned to greet his mother and the other queens. His heart stopped when he saw them wearing the simple white clothes of mourning. 'Mother,' he said as he touched Kaushalya's feet. 'What has happened? Why are you all dressed like this?'

As Kaushalya and the other queens began to wail, Shatrughna said, 'Our father has passed away, Rama. He has gone to the realm of the ancestors, secure in all the good deeds he performed during his lifetime.'

Rama fell to the ground as if struck by a bolt of lightning. His calm, bright face was shadowed with sadness, his clear eyes were dimmed with tears. He wept silently, his tears watering the earth in front of him. Lakshmana stood silent but his face, too, was clouded with grief. Sita whispered words of solace to Kaushalya and led her and the other queens to the shade of the shimshapa tree that grew in front of their little hut. Reunited as a family, the brothers, along with Sita and their mothers, prayed silently for the safe passage of Dasharatha's soul to the worlds beyond those of the ancestors and the gods.

When they had all composed themselves, Bharata spoke. 'Come back with me, Rama. Ayodhya needs a new king. Look, our entire royal court is here. So are the people. We all want you to take our father's place on the throne.'

'I cannot do that, Bharata. I am bound by the king's word. I cannot go against that,' Rama said. 'The kingdom is safe in your hands. You will be a good king because you are a good man. We all trust you,' he continued as he turned to the priests and ministers and the royal court. 'I appreciate you all coming here and bearing this difficult journey. You are my elders and my teachers, it is I who should have come to you.'

'Come back with us, Rama,' said Vasishtha, the royal priest. 'The king is dead. His wishes and commands do not need to be obeyed any more.'

'The king was also my father,' replied Rama. 'Since he is no longer with us, sending me to the forest is his last wish. It is my duty as a son to do what my father has asked of me. I do not want to argue with you, good teacher. But I am firm in my resolve. I shall live out my fourteen-year exile in the forest. You have taught me that dharma is all important.

'Go with Bharata. Teach him to be a good king, a king who cares for his people before he cares for himself, a king who ensures that even the poorest man will receive justice, a king who keeps his word, no matter the cost to himself. This is what our father, King Dasharatha, taught me. It is not easy to be the kind of king that he was, so all of you, priests and ministers and army commanders alike, must stand by Bharata. Give him the benefit of your experience and give him your loyalty. Treat him as you would your own son. Advise him well and strengthen his resolve. Guard his borders and let him be aware of all that happens in the kingdom. Remind him to be compassionate and respectful. Above all, let him never fail in his duty to his people.'

Rama turned to Bharata and said, 'Go, my brother. Ayodhya waits for you.'

'I will not sit on the throne of Ayodhya while you are still alive,' said Bharata firmly. 'I have a duty towards our people, I know that. I shall rule in your name, from outside the city. I shall enter Ayodhya along with you, fourteen years from now. Give me your sandals, Rama. They shall be the symbol of your presence, a sign that our kingdom has your blessings and that you will return to rule us all.'

Seeing that both Rama and Bharata had made up their minds and would not be persuaded otherwise, Vasishtha signalled to the others that the decision had been made. The royal court withdrew to a distance so that the king's family could be together for a little while.

As the day drew long, Bharata rose to leave. 'I will hold the kingdom in trust for you, Rama,' he said, as he touched his brother's feet. He embraced Lakshmana and bowed to Sita before he left, his eyes on the ground as he walked away.

Life in Chitrakuta continued peacefully, as before. 'I am very happy here, Rama,' said Sita one day. 'Life is so simple, so uncomplicated. We have learned so much about trees and flowers and fruits. We have learned to respect the Earth for all that she gives us. This is not what we would have learned in the city.'

'Well, your mother, the Earth, has certainly given you some fine ornaments,' smiled Rama as he slipped a bracelet of flowers on to Sita's slim wrist. 'These delicate flowers suit you, my dear.'

'But I worry about one thing,' Sita went on. 'Why do you need your weapons here, Rama? We live as ascetics, we have no need for bows and arrows and swords and shields. The birds and the animals are our friends. There are no dangers here in Chitrakuta. I fear that your weapons will bring violence to us, that you will use them because you have them with you. When we return to the city and you are king, you can arm yourself again, as a warrior and a king must. For now, why don't you put them away?'

'If only it were that simple, sweet Sita.' Rama sighed. 'I carry weapons not to protect myself, but to protect others, those who need help and those who are weak and cannot protect themselves. Sometimes, violence is necessary, if you are doing the right thing. That is the code of the warrior and I must abide by it. It was the dharma into which I was born and I must uphold it, wherever I am, whether in the forest or in the city. Besides, I have promised the sages who live in these regions that I will protect them from rakshasas and other wicked creatures. I must keep my weapons sharp and well-tended. But don't worry, I know that you will never let me lift my bow without good reason.'

As Rama and Sita and Lakshmana wandered through the pleasant meadows and groves of Chitrakuta, they reached the settlement of the great sage Agastya. He was also known as Kumbhayoni because he had been born from a pot. Agastya was pleased to see Rama and blessed him. 'I have been waiting for you, Rama,' he said. 'I have weapons that I must give you. These weapons – this great jewel-studded bow, this inexhaustible quiver of arrows, this gleaming sword – these are from the gods. Use them against your enemies, Rama, not against anyone else.' Rama looked at Sita as he accepted the weapons and she smiled, knowing that Rama had already considered what the sage was telling him to do.

'You should go further, Rama,' advised the sage. 'To fulfil the spirit of your promise to your father, you need to be far away from human settlements.'

And so, the three of them travelled onward, deeper into the dreaded Dandaka forest. All of a sudden, they heard a mighty roar, so inhuman that it made their hair stand on end. 'Get behind me, Sita,' cried Lakshmana as he reached for arrows from his quiver.

Almost before they could move, a gigantic creature crashed through the trees and charged towards them. He was dressed in animal skins that dripped with blood and fat. The vicious-looking spears he carried had the heads of elephants and tigers and wild boar impaled upon them. He swatted Lakshmana aside as if he were a fly and, in a trice, he had grabbed Sita and placed her on his broad hip.

'I cannot bear Sita being touched by anyone!' shouted Rama as he blazed with anger and let fly a rain of arrows.

Lakshmana recovered and moved in to attack the creature with his sword. All you could see were the golden tips of the arrows that flashed like lightning through the clouds of dust raised by the brothers as they weaved and ducked, attacking from all sides. It was not long before they had cut off the creature's massive arms. His body crashed to the forest floor and Sita, almost dead with fright, found herself safe with Rama again. The brothers carried Sita away from where the great creature had fallen and when they were a good distance away they sat down and caught their breath.

'These are the dangers of the forest, Lakshmana,' said Rama quietly. 'I wish we had not brought Sita with us. We've been safe so far, close to where the sages live. But as we go deeper into this dark place, we'll face more and more ghastly creatures. How are we going to protect this delicate princess?'

'Never fear, brother,' said Lakshmana. 'I am by your side. Nothing will happen to you or to your wife. I will keep my weapons in better shape than before. Now, we have to find a secure place to build our hut and settle down.'

They walked further, cautious and alert, seeking out a place that would be sheltered and also allow them to monitor all the directions, in case they were attacked again. They had all been shaken by the violent encounter, but Rama put on a cheerful face as he tried to keep Sita distracted. He talked about the little home they would build and teased her gently as she continued to tremble at the memory of being held by the monster.

Before sundown that day, they had found a peaceful spot to build their hut. It was not too far from the river but far enough from the dense forest. There was an area in front where Sita could grow her plants and feed the deer and squirrels and birds that always came to her. Plus, the hut stood on higher ground, so Rama and Lakshmana could keep watch over the area.

Although Panchavati was beautiful and serene, the sense of danger continued to hang in the air and the brothers thought it best to be on their guard. Lakshmana polished and sharpened their weapons every morning. The sword blades gleamed like silver moonlight and the tips of the arrows were as yellow-bright as the sun. The weapons lit up the corner of the hut where they were stored.

One day, Sita returned from her bath in the river and joined the brothers as they sat outside their hut, chatting about this and that – the doe who had recently given birth nearby, the best time to pick the bilva fruit from the tree by the hut, how they might keep themselves warm and dry when the rains came. Sita looked at her handsome husband and thought how lucky she was to love a man like that and have his love in return. Lakshmana, too, was a fine man and, again, she thanked the gods for all the good things she had, even though she was a princess who had to live in the forest for fourteen years.

Sita was not the only one admiring Rama at that moment. Hidden in the trees nearby stood a rakshasi. Her name was Shurpanakha and she, too, gazed at Rama with love in her eyes. She noticed his strong arms, his broad shoulders and powerful chest, his long, firm legs. She was dazzled by his clear forehead, his bright eyes shaped like the petals of a lotus, his eyebrows, dark as a crow's wing. Shurpanakha had never seen such an attractive man before and, because she was a rakshasi who lived freely and by her own rules in the forest, she decided that she wanted him for herself. She burst through the trees and bounded up to where Rama sat with his wife and his brother. All at once, it seemed as if the sun had been swallowed by a dark cloud. The breeze dropped and there was a great hush in the air.

'My name is Shurpanakha and this forest is my playground. I go wherever I want and I do whatever I please. I want you to be mine,' she said in her harsh voice. 'I don't care who you are or where you have come from!'

Rama looked at Shurpanakha, completely unperturbed. He took in her vast size, her gaping mouth filled with large teeth, her rough hair that hung down on either side of her face, her drooping belly and her sharp, yellow nails. Calmly, he told her who he was and why he was in

the forest. 'Come away with me,' she begged and held out her massive arms to him. 'I am in love with you!'

'But I am a married man,' replied Rama, standing protectively in front of Sita, who was shaking like a leaf in a storm. 'If you want a companion, why don't you ask my brother Lakshmana? He's available at the moment.'

'This is not the time to be mischievous, Rama!' shouted Lakshmana, his sword already drawn and in his hand. 'This woman is dangerous. Look at her – she's a wild thing from the forest!'

At that very moment, Shurpanakha lunged towards Sita, her clawed hands grabbing the air, her huge mouth open as if to swallow the delicate princess in a single gulp. As Sita collapsed in a faint behind him, Rama reached for his bow, yelling, 'Cut off her nose and ears, Lakshmana! Now!'

'Let me kill her, Rama!' cried Lakshmana.

'No! No!' shouted Rama in response. 'She is a woman!'

Lakshmana's sword whistled through the air, a ray from the hidden sun bouncing off its blade. In an instant, Shurpanakha was covered in dark blood, almost black, that spouted from her nose and from the sides of her face. She howled in pain and charged back into the forest, tearing off the low-hanging branches from trees, trampling on flowering bushes and crushing plants and sweet-scented grass into the ground as she ran. As her howls receded, the forest seemed to breathe again – the birds twittered nervously, the breeze returned in gusts, as if unsure whether the danger had passed, and the river's sweet song rose again.

'I'm sure that's not the last we've seen of this,' said Lakshmana as he wiped the rakshasi's blood off his sword. The princes revived Sita, sprinkling water on her face and rubbing the soles of her feet. They took her into the cool, dim interior of the hut, trying to erase the memory of the last few minutes. Sita clung to Rama, still trembling, and Rama whispered words of love and reassurance into her shell-like ears. Lakshmana bowed to their weapons and steadied his mind to recall all that Vishwamitra had taught them when they were young boys about how to power the bows and arrows and spears and swords and shields with the energy of the gods.

Shurpanakha hurtled blindly through the forest, holding her face, trying to staunch the flowing blood and snot and tears of rage with her hands. She ploughed onward until she reached Janasthana, where her brother Khara lived with an army of rakshasas, and collapsed at his feet, heaving, sobbing, bleeding, shaking with anger.

'Who has done this to you, sister?' roared Khara. He lifted her up and was horrified at her mutilated face. 'Tell me who it is! I swear that he shall not see another sunrise!'

'There are two men in the forest and they are accompanied by a woman. They say they are the princes of Ayodhya. They did this to me, they did!' sobbed Shurpanakha. 'Avenge this insult to me and to the rakshasas!'

Khara summoned fourteen of his most experienced warriors, each of whom had killed thousands of creatures, including human beings, and sent them off, armed to the teeth, to destroy the men who had harmed his sister.

Rama and Lakshmana were prepared. As the fourteen rakshasas attacked from all sides, they stood back to back, fearless. Showers of arrows flew from their bows like rain, none missing their mark. Rakshasa spears bounced off their shields and fell to the ground, useless. The princes ducked and weaved and covered each other. Before long, their bodies bathed in sweat, they stood tall amongst fourteen dead rakshasas.

As soon as Khara heard about the defeat of his prized warriors, he sent an entire army, led by his brother Dushana, to replace them. As they set out, bad omens filled the skies – a donkey-coloured cloud rained dirty water on the rakshasa troops, jackals and hyenas howled from the wilderness, fiery meteors tore through the skies at high noon. But the rakshasa army was not deterred.

Fourteen thousand rakshasas proved no match for the prince

of Ayodhya. Rama faced them alone, armed with the weapons of the gods. He clad himself in armour so bright that it blinded his opponents. When he saw the rakshasa army approaching with their battle banners fluttering in the dusty wind, Rama twanged the string of the great bow which had belonged to Vishnu. The sound ripped through the worlds, felling rakshasas on all sides. Sun-tipped arrows flew from that bow, blazing with fire as they rained upon the rakshasas.

Spears and missiles powered by the magic spells Rama had learned from Vishwamitra flew soundlessly through the air and hit their targets. Soon, fourteen thousand rakshasa corpses – pierced with arrows and spears, their weapons cracked and broken, their armour bloodied and torn – lay scattered across Janasthana. Even the gods came to watch this great battle. They stood in the sky and they clapped and cheered and rained fresh and fragrant flowers upon victorious Rama.

Shurpanakha screamed in anger when she saw her brothers – Khara, Dushana and Trishiras – all dead upon the ground. She gathered her wits and her powers and flew through the air to Lanka, ruled by the mightiest of her brothers, Ravana, lord of all the rakshasas in the three worlds.

Ravana was unlike any other rakshasa. He was the greatest of them all. He had ten heads and twenty arms. He was strong and powerful, he was learned and was a brilliant musician. He had performed such severe penances that the gods had been forced to give him boons that made him more and more invincible. He ruled in Lanka like Indra did in heaven – his palace was huge, his land was rich, his people were prosperous and happy. And he owned the magical chariot Pushpaka which could fly through the air, following the thoughts of those who rode in it. Pushpaka could go anywhere that the heart desired and the mind imagined. But Ravana was arrogant – he believed that nothing and no one could stop him from getting what he wanted.

Shurpanakha barged into Ravana's court, her eyes blazing. 'Look! Look!' she wailed, showing her brother her mutilated face. 'How can you sit here and watch dancing girls when I have been treated like this! Get up! Do something! There is obviously someone in the world who has no fear of you if they could do this to me!'

Ravana shook himself and adjusted his ten crowns upon his ten heads. 'What are you talking about? Who is there in the three worlds that does not fear me!' he roared.

'Rama has just killed fourteen thousand rakshasas, including our brothers Khara, Dushana and Trishiras. He fought them alone. Get up Ravana, your death is at hand,' said Shurpanakha.

'Don't talk rubbish, sister. Who is this Rama? Where does he come from? Where is he now?' roared Ravana, his twenty eyes blazing with anger.

'Rama is the prince of Ayodhya. He has been exiled into the forest for fourteen years with his wife and his brother,' said Shurpanakha more calmly, now that she had Ravana's attention. 'His brother is also very powerful and a skilled warrior – he is the one who cut off my nose and ears.

'But you should see Rama's wife,' she continued slyly. 'Sita is beautiful, the loveliest woman in the world. She has skin the colour of gold, her hair is dark and long and falls to her waist like the shadow of night. Her face is softer and more delicate than the bloom of the morning lotus. Ravana, a woman like that should belong to you. If you kill those violent men, Rama and his brother, Sita can be yours!'

'Hmm,' grunted Ravana and he dismissed his sister and all of his court. Ravana could not bear the thought that there was something beautiful that did not belong to him. His palace was already filled with the finest women in the three worlds – the daughters of the gods, of daityas and danavas, and gandharvas and uragas and pannagas. 'There's always room for one more,' he thought to himself as he summoned Pushpaka and told the magical chariot to take him to his uncle Maricha.

Maricha trembled when he saw Ravana approaching, for he feared his nephew and his ambitions. He bowed and offered him water to wash his feet as the mighty king of the rakshasas dismounted from his magnificent vehicle.

'Maricha, I look after you. You cannot refuse me anything. I am going to abduct this beautiful Sita and I have a plan that involves you. Turn yourself into a golden deer and draw Rama deep into the forest and I will carry his wife away. Sita will be mine. If I have to return to kill Rama and his brother, I shall. What do I have to worry about these weak and powerless human beings!'

'Ah Ravana! Do not make an enemy of Rama,' begged Maricha. 'He is not a human like the others. He is special, the gods love him. Your enmity with him could be the end of the rakshasas, the end of your great kingdom, the end of you, even. Go back to your pleasure gardens and your women, Ravana. Let Sita be. Let Rama be. Listen to my words!'

'You coward!' shouted Ravana. 'Come on! Climb into Pushpaka! I have no time to waste and no interest in your ridiculous fears. If the gods loved Rama, would he be in exile in the forest? A homeless wanderer, sleeping on leaves and eating roots and shoots, dragging his wife and his brother behind him?'

Sita was scattering crumbs for the birds in front of the hut as she did every day, waiting for her little friends to come and eat, shake their feathers and bathe in the water she had put out for them. Suddenly, she saw a flash from the corner of her eye. She looked around and there, just ahead of the flowers she had planted, she saw a deer. It pawed the ground, it stretched its neck, it nibbled at the grass, it pranced and danced. The deer shimmered in the sun, golden on one side and silver on the other. Its hooves sparkled like diamonds, its eyes flashed like dark sapphires, its horns shone like polished onyx.

'Rama! Lakshmana!' she called out in delight. 'Come and look at this deer! I've never seen one like it. Oh, I must have it. Catch it for me!'

Rama came up from the river and Lakshmana stopped polishing his weapons and came to where Sita was.

'Do you really want it, my darling?' asked Rama. 'It shouldn't be hard to capture. I'll fetch it for you.'

'Stop, Rama!' said Lakshmana. 'This has to be a trick. This is no ordinary deer, look at it. The rakshasas are waiting to take revenge for what we did the other day. They can take any form they choose, become anything they want. Do not go after this creature.'

The deer came closer and then danced away. It seemed to be asking Rama to follow, skipping between the trees, now hiding itself, now becoming visible, like a streak of lightning playing in the monsoon clouds.

'Lakshmana, you have been away from home too long. You see danger everywhere. It's just a deer. I'm going to catch it,' said Rama. He picked up his bow and his quiver and moved quickly towards the edge of the forest where the deer stood, waiting. 'Sita, this deer shall be yours!' he cried as he followed the deer into the dark shadow of the trees. 'Don't leave Sita alone, Lakshmana. I'll be back before you know it.'

'Get inside the hut, Sita,' said Lakshmana roughly. 'I am worried, I sense that we are not safe.'

Lakshmana sought out his weapons and armed himself, ushering Sita into the hut. But even before she had entered there, a voice rang out in the distance. 'Oooo Lakshmana! Sitaaaa!'

Sita stopped in her tracks, struck with panic. 'That's Rama's voice! He is in danger, Lakshmana. Go to him. Help him. Bring my beloved Rama back to me!' she cried.

'Sita, this is rakshasa magic. That was not a real deer. This is not Rama's voice,' said Lakshmana, though his bow was at the ready.

'It was a deer, this is Rama's voice, I would know his voice anywhere,' wept Sita. 'O Lakshmana, I beg you, save your brother!'

'I can't go after him, I cannot leave you here with no protection,' said Lakshmana as calmly as he could. He could feel a great wave of tension rising up from his feet to his head. Something was terribly wrong, he knew it.

'I cannot live without Rama,' said Sita, her face streaked with tears. 'I'll stay inside the hut, I promise you. Please, please, go after your brother and help him!'

'All right,' said Lakshmana. 'Do not leave the hut, do not step beyond your garden, whatever happens. Even if you hear me shouting for help!' He ran into the forest, following the footsteps of Rama and the golden deer.

Sita went inside the hut, wiping her tears, praying for the safety of her beloved husband and his brave brother. She begged the deities of the forest and her mother, the Earth, that they should both return to her, unharmed.

A little while later, she heard someone calling out. 'Mother, mother!' said the voice. It sounded old and tired. She peeped out of the hut and saw a man, bent with age, carrying a wooden staff and an iron pot. Without a second thought, Sita dipped her ladle into the clay water jar that Lakshmana had made for her and carried it outside, offering it to the old man who stood before her, dressed in the ragged robes of a wandering mendicant.

'Are you hungry? Can I give you something to eat?' she asked kindly.

'Yes, please,' the old voice quavered.

Sita went inside the hut and gathered up some fruit. She held it out to the old man, but he said, 'I am so tired. Please bring it to me.'

Sita stepped out, crossing the bed of flowers at the edge of her garden. She reached over to place the fruit in the bowl that he held out, unmindful of Lakshmana's warning to stay inside her garden.

In a trice, the old man flung back his robe. Ten-headed Ravana stretched his twenty arms towards Sita and swept her up. His laughter rang through the trees as he called Pushpaka to him. Sita screamed, 'Rama! Rama! Lakshmana! Where are you? Help me!' but Ravana had her by the waist and he tossed her over his shoulder as he climbed into his magical chariot.

'There is no one here to help you, my pretty!' he cried as he urged Pushpaka to rise into the skies above the forest. 'Rama is a mere mortal. I am Ravana, the king of the rakshasas! There's nothing he can do to get you back.'

Golden-skinned Sita wept and wailed and writhed in Ravana's dark arms as Pushpaka rose above the trees. Pushpaka created a mighty wind as it tore through the skies and the sound of Ravana's cruel laughter rumbled through the worlds like thunder before a storm. On the ground below, deer and rabbits and squirrels followed Pushpaka's shadow, their eyes fixed on their gentle friend who was being borne away. Trees swayed and stretched out their branches as if to reclaim Sita from her captor. Bushes and grass seemed to weep, unable to bear the sight of Sita being wrenched from her forest hut and her quiet life. 'Faster, faster!' shouted Ravana to Pushpaka, holding Sita as the flowers from her hair and neck and wrists fell like rain.

Resting in the trees in the heart of the forest was the great vulture Jatayu. One of the finest warriors that the three worlds had ever known, Jatayu was a friend of King Dasharatha. He was old now and lived away from humans, resting his weary wings and eating whatever he found close by. But his eyes and ears were still sharp and he knew everything that happened in the lands around him. He heard a great disturbance and when he looked up he saw a chariot flying high above him.

There seemed to be a woman in the chariot and he could hear her cries of distress. 'Could that be Sita? I know she is here in the forest with Rama and Lakshmana,' he thought to himself. With a single thrust of his enormous wings, Jatayu rose upwards, scanning the skies around him. He recognized Pushpaka and knew that it belonged to the king of the rakshasas. His heart beat faster as he flew closer. He knew that whoever was with Ravana in the chariot, it was someone that did not want to be there.

Jatayu moved into the path of Pushpaka, his great wings flapping, his sharp beak and claws at the ready. 'Stop!' he called. 'Who is there and who are you with?'

'Get away, you old fool,' bellowed Ravana. 'Go back and sleep in the forest. This is no place for you!' and he drove Pushpaka straight at the bird.

'Help! I am Sita, Rama's wife!' cried Sita, hoping that this enormous vulture was a friend rather than a foe.

Jatayu swooped down on the chariot and attacked Ravana with his claws. Ravana pulled out his sword and slashed at him wildly. Jatayu wheeled and turned and dived, attacking Ravana's twenty arms and ten heads with his sharp beak. Ravana's black blood flowed from the wounds that Jatayu inflicted but the rakshasa's mighty arms, each wielding a deadly weapon, soon overpowered the ageing bird. Ravana cut through Jatayu's wings and the great bird crashed through the treetops to the ground. The earth shook when he fell, and he lay there, straining for his last breaths. 'You will pay for this, Ravana,' he croaked. 'Rama will be your death!'

Ravana paid no heed and flew onward to Lanka.

Meanwhile, Lakshmana stumbled through the forest, trying to find Rama and the deer. He ran through groves and clearings, slashing at creepers and vines, tripping over roots as he called out to his brother. Panting and out of breath, his mind teetered between his concern for Sita, whom he had left alone, and his fear for what had happened to Rama. But he ran on, his bow strapped to his shoulder. Suddenly, he saw Rama standing in a clearing, a twisted rakshasa body at his feet. 'Rama!' he cried. 'You're safe! What is this? Where's the deer?'

'You were right, Lakshmana. It was a rakshasa. As soon as my arrow pierced the deer, it called out to you in my voice. And this ghastly rakshasa emerged from within its body. He's dead now. So we are out of danger. Oh no!' he said, as he looked around. 'You didn't leave Sita alone, did you?'

Lakshmana nodded miserably.

'How could you do that? You know there are rakshasas around! Anything could have happened to her!' Rama began to run even before he finished speaking, heading back towards the little hut where they had all been so happy.

Ignoring the branches that slapped his face, the thorns that scratched his arms and the stones that lay in his path, Rama ran helter-skelter back to the hut.

Lakshmana was behind him, but Rama had eyes only for what awaited him. 'Sita! Sita!' he shouted, looking here and there, inside the hut and outside, among the flowers, by the river, even among the trees. 'She's gone, Lakshmana! Someone has taken her,' he cried as he fell to the ground, weeping as if his heart had broken into a thousand pieces. 'I care nothing for the loss of my kingdom, Lakshmana, but the loss of Sita is something that I cannot bear!'

The Monkey Kingdom

Lakshmana ran to his brother and raised him up from the ground. 'Do not despair, Rama. I promise you, we will bring Sita back. Wherever she is, we will find her. Whoever has taken her, we will destroy him! I swear this on my honour as a warrior! Come, now. Pull yourself together, we cannot delay.'

Rama closed his eyes. He steadied his breathing and focused his mind. He said softly, 'Blessed deities of the forest, blessed trees and plants and flowers and animals. Sita loved you all and you loved her. You saw what happened in my absence, you know who took her. Help me find my beloved Sita.'

He opened his eyes and said, 'This way, Lakshmana. I feel sure that whoever took Sita went in this direction.'

Swiftly, the brothers moved through the forest, their eyes peeled, their senses alert. They saw flowers, damaged and bruised, strewn along the forest floor. Before long, they heard someone or something moaning and breathing heavily. They ran towards the sound and came upon mighty Jatayu, the great vulture who had tried to save Sita, lying in a clearing.

Rama ran to him. 'Jatayu! Friend of my father! Who has done this to you?'

Jatayu moved his head wearily, blood trickling from his mouth. 'Ah, Rama, I am sorry that you see me like this.' He sighed. 'I tried to stop a chariot in the sky. A woman was being carried away against her will. But I was struck down, Rama. I fear these are my last moments on earth.'

'That woman was my wife,' cried Rama. 'Please, Jatayu, who carried her off? Where is he taking her? Can you remember, can you tell me?' he pleaded.

'It must have been Ravana, king of the rakshasas,' whispered the old bird. 'No one else has a flying chariot like that. May my last words help you in your quest!' he said with his dying breath.

Rama and Lakshmana buried noble Jatayu, giving him the same respect and honour they would have given their father. But without lingering, they set off in a southerly direction to find Sita. They hurried along, barely stopping to eat or rest, hoping to find something that would indicate to them where Sita had gone. Alarmingly close to them, they heard a deep rumble in the trees and they held their weapons at the ready.

Before their eyes, a great creature emerged, unlike anything they had seen before – his body was headless, his enormous mouth studded with yellowing teeth sat in the middle of his vast stomach, his legs were like tree trunks and each of his arms was a mile long. His voice seemed to come from the skies as he bellowed, 'Who are you and where are you going? The gods of the forest have sent you to me as food – you will not get past me!'

The rakshasa stretched out his mighty arms to capture the princes but they slashed at them in the same way they had attacked the forest creature who had picked up Sita so long ago. Bleeding profusely and stumbling in confusion with the pain from his wounds, the rakshasa fell to his knees.

'We are warriors,' said Rama. 'I am Rama, prince of Ayodhya, Dasharatha's son. And I have no fear of you.'

'I have been waiting for you,' said the rakshasa with a sigh. 'My name is Kabandha. I was not always this horrible, deformed being. Burn this body for me and I will tell you what you need to know!'

The brothers carried Kabandha over to a sheltered hollow and prepared a funeral pyre. Shining like the sun, tall and straight as a sala tree, Kabandha rose out of the flames in his original form. 'I know you are searching for your wife, who has been abducted by Ravana. You will need an ally to get her back. Go and make friendship with Sugriva. He is the exiled king of the monkeys of Kishkindha, who are strong and powerful. He is the friend you need.'

'Please do not delay. Tell me where I will find Sugriva,' cried Rama, his eyes filled with tears at the thought of Sita in captivity somewhere far away.

'Go west from here, Rama,' said Kabandha. 'When the forest ends, you will come to a beautiful lake called Pampa, filled with birds and lotus blossoms. To the east of the lake is the Rishyamuka mountain. Sugriva lives there with his ministers. Find him and make an alliance with him.' Kabandha flew into the sky, his voice fading as he disappeared above the treetops.

Rama and Lakshmana turned westward and were guided by the sun as they travelled to the outer edge of the Dandaka forest and onward to Kishkindha.

From a low hilltop in a rocky region that was filled with caves and lakes and hidden sources of water, a group of monkeys watched the princes enter their lands. 'Who can they be?' they said to each other.

'They are armed like warriors but they wear the clothes of ascetics.'

Sugriva was the leader of this small band that had made its home on the Rishyamuka mountain. His most trusted companion was Hanuman, son of Vayu, the wind god. 'Go and find out who they are and what they want, Hanuman,' Sugriva said to him. 'We do not see men like this here.'

In the blink of an eye, moving faster than thought, Hanuman had leapt off the mountain and was standing before Rama and Lakshmana. He bowed to them and said, 'I am Hanuman, son of the Wind. My master is Sugriva and we live there, on the Rishyamuka mountain. Who are you and what brings you to Kishkindha, land of the monkeys?'

Rama looked at Hanuman and saw a monkey, brave and tall and fearless. 'I am Rama, prince of Ayodhya, son of Dasharatha. This is my brother, Lakshmana. My wife has been abducted by Ravana, king of the rakshasas. We seek the help of your master, Sugriva. Can you take us to him?'

Hanuman lifted the princes on to his shoulders and bounded

across the rocks and up the steep slope of Rishyamuka, setting them down in front of Sugriva. He introduced Rama and Sugriva to each other and then stood back, wary and watchful, along with Lakshmana.

'I have been sent to you, Sugriva. I was told that you can help me find my wife who has been stolen by the king of the rakshasas. Tell me, will you be my ally?' said Rama, bluntly, not wanting to waste any time.

'Prince of Ayodhya, we can make a pact,' said Sugriva, shrewdly. 'Help me and I will help you.'

'Anything you ask,' said Rama.

'Very well,' said Sugriva, offering Rama a seat made of grass. 'I live here on this forsaken mountain with my few followers because my brother Vali exiled me from the kingdom of Kishkindha. Listen, and I will tell you my story.

'My older brother Vali ruled all the monkeys of this great land from the city of Kishkindha. One day, a terrible demon arrived at our city gates and challenged Vali to a fight. They fought long and hard, over days. Their combat took them over hills and into valleys, across lakes and rivers and into caves. I was afraid for my brother and I followed him, hoping that I could be of help. After a while, Vali and the demon descended into a huge cave. I stood outside, waiting. After many days, I heard a ghastly scream and blood began to pour out of the cave's mouth, right beneath my feet. I was sure that my brother had been killed and I moved a huge rock over the entrance of the cave to trap that horrible monster so that he would not emerge and harm our people. I ran back to our city and told everyone what had happened. I was weeping and exhausted, my heart broken because I was sure that my brother had been killed.

'The monkey ministers and citizens installed me as king in Vali's place and I ruled for a while. But then, one day, Vali reappeared. He accused me of trying to kill him by closing off the cave's entrance. He said that I had taken the kingdom from him and, as a younger brother, I had no right to rule while he was still alive. Nothing I said could persuade him otherwise. He even took my wife before he banished me from Kishkindha. These few loyal monkeys came with me, knowing the truth of my thoughts and deeds.

'Help me get my kingdom and my wife back. Kill Vali and I will summon hundreds and thousands of mighty monkeys and bears to find your wife. They will go to the four corners of the earth and will not rest until they have found her. Then, we shall make a great army and bring her back. What do you say, Rama?'

Rama did not hesitate and held out his hand. 'Let fire be the witness to our eternal friendship, Sugriva. I will do as you ask in return for your help.'

'But how do I know that you are Vali's equal? What if he is a greater warrior than you? After all, you are a human. And Vali's father is Indra, the king of the gods,' said Sugriva.

Rama said nothing but drew his bow and pulled a sure and sharp arrow from his quiver. The arrow flew through the air, silent as breath. It pierced through a row of seven sala trees, one after the other, and returned to Rama, who caught it in one hand. Sugriva bowed and touched Rama's feet. 'Forgive me for doubting you, Rama. It is I who shall be privileged to be your ally.'

'Call Vali out tomorrow. Tell him you want to fight him. I shall hide behind this tree and wait for the right moment to kill him.'

The next morning, Sugriva went to the gates of Kishkindha and called Vali out to fight. Vali said to Sugriva, 'What are you doing? You know you cannot defeat me in battle. Do you want to die, foolish monkey?'

'Your arrogance will kill you, Vali,' replied Sugriva. 'Come to where the land is flat and we shall fight!'

A terrible fight began between the monkey brothers. They used their teeth and nails to attack each other, scratching and biting and drawing blood. They hit each other with their fists and their feet, they threw stones and rocks at each other, they uprooted trees and hurled them through the air. They grunted and growled and the earth shook with the force of their blows.

Rama watched silently from behind a tree, his bow fitted with a sharp arrow. Soon, it became clear that Vali was getting the upper hand. Sugriva reeled from a blow to his chest and withdrew from the fight, his head spinning. As he ran away, Vali laughed and shouted, 'Run, little brother! You are no match for me!'

Sugriva stumbled into the shadow of Rishyamuka where his followers were waiting for him. They attended to his wounds and bruises and wiped the blood from his face. 'What a fine friend you are, Rama,' he panted. 'Where were you? Why didn't you do something? I'm half dead because of you!'

'I couldn't tell which one was you, Sugriva. You and Vali look exactly alike. I couldn't take the chance of killing you,' replied Rama.

'Well, what are we going to do, then?' said Sugriva with fear in his eyes.

'Call Vali out again tomorrow. I will make no mistake. Lakshmana, put that flowering creeper around Sugriva's neck, like a garland. I will be able to identify him with that,' said Rama.

The next morning, Sugriva, wearing the garland of flowers, challenged Vali again. Vali swaggered out of the city gates, confident

that he would defeat Sugriva easily. Once more, the brothers fought, locked hand to hand, foot to foot, forehead to forehead. They heaved and twisted and threw each other to the ground. Then, an arrow whizzed through the air and hit Vali in the back. He collapsed at once, pulling Sugriva on top of him. Sugriva struggled to his feet and stood there, looking down at his dying brother.

'Who did this to me?' said Vali. 'Who shot me in the back when I was fighting another opponent? This is not just, this is not right!'

Rama emerged from behind the tree and came up to Vali. 'I am Rama, prince of Ayodhya, son of Dasharatha. I have killed you because of what you have done to your brother. You took his wife and you banished him from the kingdom. He is younger than you, you should have treated him like a son. It is your own actions that brought about your death, Vali.'

'But, Rama, you always do the right thing. I have heard about you. You stand firm in dharma. How could you shoot me in the back when you were hidden, when I was fighting another? Surely that was wrong,' said Vali.

'You are a monkey, Vali,' snapped Rama. 'What do you know of what is right and what is wrong, about what is dharma and what is not? How can you question me about what I did? Sugriva and I have a pact of friendship. His enemy is my enemy. It is too late for you to argue or to question what happened.'

'Ah! One cannot see where one's actions lead. It was my fate to be killed by you, Rama.' Vali sighed. 'But I can try and make up for what I did. Sugriva, take my only son, Angada. Look after him as if he were your own, treat him well, as I never treated you. Let him be king of the monkeys after you. Look after my wife, she has no one. The sun is growing dim, I must go now, to the lands of our fathers.' Vali clasped Sugriva's hand as he took his last breath.

'Vali was a king, Sugriva,' said Rama. 'We must give him a royal funeral before we crown you king of Kishkindha. Remember what Vali asked of you – treat Angada as if he were your own son.'

The monkeys sadly buried their king and went back to the city of Kishkindha for the coronation.

'The rainy season will soon be upon us, Rama,' said Sugriva, the new king of Kishkindha. 'I promise to call the great monkeys and bears together when the rains end. Then, we will begin the search for Sita.'

Rama and Lakshmana retired to a cave among the rocks of Kishkindha, waiting impatiently for the season to change. Each day, Rama grew more and more sad. The rains made him think of Sita. Her hair was as dark as the thunderclouds, the lightning flashes were the colour of her skin, the raindrops on the leaves were her laughter – everything around him reminded Rama of his beloved wife. Lakshmana did his best to keep his brother cheerful, but there was not much that he could do.

After months that seemed like years to Rama, he saw that the heavy rain clouds had become lighter and were being pushed away by the wind. Trees and flowers and small animals shook themselves, turning their faces towards the sun, who had returned to his rightful place, shining brightly in the middle of the sky. Lizards came out to warm themselves on rocks, birds sang a different song, the earth seemed refreshed. Rivers slithered back to their usual courses like snakes returning to their homes.

Rama felt a renewed sense of purpose and said to Lakshmana, 'Go to Kishkindha and tell Sugriva that I am ready. It is time for him to fulfil his promise to me. The rains are over. It's time to find Sita!'

Lakshmana arrived at the gates of the monkey city. He roared, 'Sugriva! Call the monkeys at your command. Rama is waiting. Make good your promise to help us find Sita, or you'll be very sorry!'

He didn't have to wait for long before Sugriva appeared. He looked like he had spent the rainy months enjoying himself – he had put on weight, his clothes were rich and splendid, his eyes were bloodshot.

'I am at your service, Lakshmana,' he growled. 'Bring Rama and meet me under those trees. I will show you what I am worth.'

As Rama and Lakshmana approached the grove that Sugriva had pointed out, they felt the earth tremble beneath their feet.

The sky darkened and a loud chattering and whooping filled the air. Everywhere they looked, they saw monkeys – hundreds and thousands of monkeys, big and small, grey, brown, white and black, even yellow. Some had red faces, others had tails that were six feet long, still others were as large as mountains. They came through the air and on the ground. They laughed and talked as they tripped over roots and brushed the branches of trees from their faces. They pulled up flowering plants and ate them. They stopped at pools to drink and splashed and played in the water.

Suddenly, a deep voice boomed out from under the trees. 'My faithful monkey chiefs, thank you for coming here with your people. We have a special task at hand, a task that will ensure that the name of our people will live forever! Are you with me?'

The monkeys shouted and clapped and roared and stamped their feet. Sugriva held up his hand for silence. 'This is my friend Rama, prince of Ayodhya, son of Dasharatha. He has been exiled from his kingdom for fourteen years. While he was in the Dandaka forest, his wife was carried away by the king of the rakshasas. I have promised him that we will find her. And then, along with our friends the bears, we will put together a mighty army, the likes of which the worlds have never seen. And we will fight the rakshasas. We will defeat them and we will bring Rama's wife back!'

Again, the monkeys cheered and whistled and thumped their chests. 'I will send the best of you out as scouts in four different directions – north, south, east and west. You have a month to find Sita. If you fail, do not bother to come back. There is no place for you in my kingdom!' roared Sugriva. 'Let the monkey leaders come to me for instructions.'

Rama and Lakshmana exchanged glances. Rama allowed a small smile to flicker across his face. Perhaps help really was at hand – he was impressed with the show of strength mustered by Sugriva. Lakshmana felt Rama's energy had changed, with hope replacing despair in his brother's heart. He reached out and touched Rama's shoulder and gave a slight nod.

Sugriva gathered his chieftains around him and divided them into four groups, giving each group a direction to search. He dispatched them swiftly to the north and the east and the west. Then he paused and said thoughtfully, 'For some reason, I believe that Sita has been taken south. I have retained my most trusted companions to explore that region. Hanuman! Take Angada, son of Vali, with you. Let him be the leader of the southern expedition. But watch him carefully, give him the benefit of your experience and your wisdom. Jambavan, the wise old bear, will also be in your group. Look to him for advice when you need it.'

Hanuman bowed to Sugriva and then went over to seek Rama's good wishes and blessings for the journey. Rama had tears in his eyes when he embraced the monkey. 'I know that you will find Sita and return to me with good news,' he said as he took off his signet ring. 'Take my ring and give it to Sita when you find her. Then she will know that you have come from me, that you are my messenger. Go safely, travel far and come back soon.'

Hanuman and Angada gathered their troop of monkeys and set off towards the south. Hanuman went ahead and Angada brought up the rear. The monkeys, who were all sons of gods and gandharvas, were in great spirits and eager for adventure. They jumped from tree to tree, they decorated themselves with garlands made from leaves and flowers, they plucked sweet fruits and shared them with one another.

They left the rocks and hills of Kishkindha and they crossed rivers and meadows and forests. Soon, the lands they knew were far behind them and they entered regions that were not so pleasant. The mountains loomed large and dark, casting their shadows over the barren earth. Dry winds created dust storms that blinded the great monkeys. But they travelled on and on.

Now, the forests they entered were not like the ones they were used to. Here, the trees grew tall, covering the sky with their intertwined branches. Thick vines hung from them and the forest floor was slippery with moss. There were no birds who sang or fruit or edible roots.

The monkeys grew tired and weary. They were hungry and they missed their homes and families. 'O, why did we start on this adventure?' they cried. 'We are lost and we are hungry. We can't even go back home as Sugriva will kill us for failing in our mission. What shall we do now? Angada, you are our leader. Help us!'

Angada looked at Hanuman. 'Do not worry, my friends,' said the son of the Wind. 'I am sure we are close to our goal. Look over there. I see the light is brighter. We can't be far from the edge of the forest. Don't lose heart now!'

The monkeys trudged along, not quite believing Hanuman. But sure enough, the trees began to thin, the light grew brighter and soon they could even see the sky. The mossy ground beneath their feet changed to a sandy soil and they could hear a booming sound in the distance. To their great surprise, they found themselves on the edge of a huge ocean whose waves crashed and pounded along the shore.

The monkeys were terrified, they had never seen the ocean before and they were certain that these great walls of water that rose and fell were the mansions of sea monsters. They huddled together, seeming nothing at all like the brave and adventurous monkeys that had left Kishkindha. Slowly, despair spread among them and they decided, one by one, to lie down on the sand and wait for death to come and take them away. There was nothing either Hanuman or Angada could do to lift their spirits, for they, too, were surprised by the ocean.

Not far from the shore, a wingless old bird had been watching the monkeys. His name was Sampati and he was Jatayu's brother. Sampati had lost his wings when he was young. One day, he and Jatayu flew high into the sky, higher than they had ever flown before. Jatayu wanted to circle the sun but as he grew close to it his wings began to burn. Sampati, the elder one, in a great burst of speed flew higher than his brother to protect him from the sun's sharp rays. Jatayu was saved, but Sampati's wings were burned off. He fell to the ground, unable to fly any longer. He ate whatever was near him, but he was often hungry.

On this day, Sampati could not believe his good fortune. 'Surely the gods still love me,' he thought as he saw the monkey hordes lie down on the beach. 'Look how much food they have sent me!' He shuffled over to where they were lying and all the monkeys screamed and ran as far as they could, convinced that a monster had come to finish them off.

Jambavan went over and spoke to the bird. 'Sampati, my old friend, we have not met since we were young! What are you doing, frightening these monkeys who are on a great mission? We'll share the food and water we have found with you. Sit and talk to me, let me tell you why we are all here,' he said.

Sampati was surprised to see his old friend and went and sat with him. Jambavan continued, 'We are trying to find Sita, the wife of Rama, prince of Ayodhya. She was carried away from the Dandaka forest by the king of the rakshasas. In fact, your brother Jatayu tried to stop him and save the princess, but Ravana killed him. Can you help us find him?'

Sampati wept noisily for his dead brother but then calmed himself and said, 'I saw a woman being carried through the air in a flying chariot. She was screaming and wailing. I thought to myself, that must be Ravana and he must be taking that poor woman to his own city, the city of Lanka which lies right in the middle of this ocean. It's very hard to reach, you know.'

The monkeys had all gathered around now, seeing that there was no danger to them from Sampati. They listened as Sampati went on to say that the only way to reach Lanka was to leap over miles and miles and then more miles of ocean.

That created a great commotion among the monkeys. 'I can leap ten yojanas,' cried one. 'I can leap twenty,' cried another, pushing him aside. 'Thirty, thirty, I can do thirty,' yelled a smaller monkey. 'Fifty!' roared a huge dark monkey with a long tail.

'Oh, it's much more than fifty yojanas,' said Sampati. 'We need someone who can jump one hundred.'

'I think I can manage about seventy yojanas,' said Angada, doubtfully.

'Why are you sitting there so quiet, Hanuman?' said Jambavan. 'You are the one that can leap these one hundred yojanas and then come back!'

'Really?' said Hanuman. 'I didn't know that.'

'You have special powers, Hanuman. You are not like the other monkeys. Let me tell you about yourself,' said Jambavan. 'You are the son of Vayu, the wind god. He promised your mother Anjana that the son that he gave her would be strong and powerful like himself. He would be fearless, as swift as the wind and a great warrior.

'One day, when you were a little baby, Hanuman, your mother left you alone as she went to the river to bathe. You were asleep but when you woke up you were hungry. You saw the sun rising, looking like a big, round, juicy fruit. You leapt towards it, Hanuman, flying through the sky with all your father's speed and power. You wanted to grab that juicy fruit and eat it and so you flew higher and faster. But, Rahu, the eclipse, had been given permission to gobble up the sun on that same day. He saw you and went running to Indra, king of the gods. "Indra, Indra," he cried. "Some other fellow is about to eat up the sun! You gave me the sun as my food! Stop him!"

'Indra pulled out his mighty thunderbolt and hurled it through the air. It struck you and you fell to the earth and broke your jaw.

Vayu was enraged that you, his young son, had been struck down by Indra. He disappeared into a cave and stopped blowing. How all the living beings in the three worlds suffered! Their limbs became stiff and as hard as wood, they could scarcely breathe. Plants and birds and animals also suffered without the gentle breeze.

'Finally, all the living beings and the gods went to Brahma, the grandfather of the worlds. They fell at his feet and begged him to appease Vayu, to get him to blow through the worlds again. "Look at how all the creatures suffer," Brahma said to Vayu. "What can we do to make you happy? Shall we all give your son boons so that he will be the mightiest monkey that ever lived? Will that please you?" he asked gently.

'Brahma laid you in his lap. As soon as he touched you, Hanuman, you revived, like a flower sprinkled with water. The gods rejoiced and each of them gave you boons – magical weapons, great strength and a quick intelligence, immense courage and freedom from harm by fire and water. You are the most powerful monkey in the world, Hanuman! It is now time for you to use your special talents and help

Rama achieve his purpose. You can leap to the island of Lanka. Do it now!'

Hanuman shook himself, as if waking from a dream. He stood up and began to expand in size. His chest filled out, his limbs pulsed with muscles, his tail waved in the air like a battle banner. He roared and thumped his chest with his fists and pounded the sands with his sturdy feet. In a flash, the great monkey had climbed to the top of a hill on the shore and he stood there, looking out over the heaving ocean. Hanuman slapped his tail on the ground and it resounded through the air like a whiplash. 'Wait for me!' he shouted to his monkey companions. 'I know that I will return successful!'

The monkeys, large in size and powerful warriors themselves, clapped and shouted as Hanuman pressed down upon the mountain which groaned under his weight as he prepared to leap into the open skies. He rose into the air, his arms outstretched, his legs spread out behind him, his great tail curled above his head. His eyes gleamed like stars, his body shone like a bolt of lightning as he flew upwards, piercing the clouds and disappearing from sight.

Hanuman looked straight ahead as he flew, his mind focused, his heart steady. He knew he had to find an island in the middle of the vast ocean, an island with a great city that was ruled by Ravana, the rakshasa who had abducted Sita. He felt no fear or restlessness, he was sure that he would know what to do when the time came. He flew past the moon and the planets and past the places where the heavenly beings lived. He flew higher than the highest mountains and whitest clouds. He flew steadily over the vast waters with the Wind, his father, pushing him gently from behind.

Suddenly, an enormous rakshasi rose up from the ocean, her massive mouth wide open, her sharp teeth bared in a smile. 'I am Surasa,' she said in a voice that boomed through the heavens. 'You have to enter my mouth, monkey! That is the boon given to me by the gods so that I am never hungry.'

'I am on a mission for Rama,' replied Hanuman calmly. 'Let me reach Lanka and find Sita. I promise that I will enter your mouth on my way back.'

'Now!' shouted Surasa, churning the waves with her huge hands and feet. 'I am hungry now!'

In the blink of an eye, Hanuman had made himself as small as a fly. He flew in and out of Surasa's mouth, through her pointed teeth and around her lolling orange tongue. He stood in the air before her and bowed with his palms joined. 'There, Surasa,' he said, 'I have entered your mouth and honoured the wishes of the gods. I'll be on my way now.' Surasa was left with her mouth hanging open, her enormous stomach empty, as the monkey, now gigantic again, flew onward.

Hanuman flew lower and scoured the surface of the ocean for an island. He felt something tugging at him and looked around. A monster, another huge rakshasi, had caught hold of his shadow that had fallen on the restless water. 'Now what?' he said to himself as he tried to get free. 'Could this be Simhika, the lion-like rakshasi, who eats creatures by swallowing their shadows?'

Up through the waves rose the largest thing Hanuman had ever seen in his life. Her hair was tawny, the colour of a lion's mane. Her hands ended in cruel claws, her eyes were the colour of amber, and her stinking mouth was open wide with her yellow fangs bared.

Quick as a flash, Hanuman entered her yawning mouth and flew down into her body. He tore up her organs and her intestines and her bladder with his nails and pounded her body with his fists. With a great hissing and sighing, like a balloon losing its air, the massive creature collapsed under the waves and sank to the bottom of the ocean, never to be seen again.

Hanuman flew onward, keeping an eye on the water below him. At last, in the distance, he saw an island, dark and brooding, that pierced through the surface of the ocean. 'That must be Lanka,' he thought to himself. 'I've certainly come far enough, about one hundred yojanas, I would say.'

He landed gently on the forbidding island, below the great peak that guarded its southern shore. He shrank to the size of a cat and, as the white moon rose into the sky, he crept into the shadows of the palace walls and looked for a way to enter Lanka, the great city of Ravana, the rakshasa king.

Lanka

Hanuman slipped through a crack in the city wall, careful to stay in the shadows as the moon poured its light over the rakshasa city. He looked around him in amazement. There were towers higher than mountain peaks, the city walls were as thick as tree trunks, red-gold lights glowed from the windows of dark buildings. 'I must remember how Lanka is laid out and where the fortifications are,' he told himself. 'That information will be useful to Rama when we attack the city.'

He saw rakshasas everywhere – the men were strong with large chests and long arms and sturdy legs. They fought with clubs and maces and they carried their shields strapped across their backs. Hanuman saw rakshasa women as well, who were beautiful and walked with ease and confidence even though the streets were dark and narrow. The monkey crept along, making his way towards Ravana's palace which lay at the centre of the city. In a short while, he came to the palace gates which were guarded by heavily armed rakshasas. But they didn't notice when a tiny monkey, the size of a cat, slipped past them and entered the royal enclosure.

Hanuman climbed quickly to the top of the upper level so that he could survey the palace. Everywhere he looked there was gold and silver and glittering jewels. The palace floor was made of crystal that gleamed like liquid moonlight, the pillars were made of beaten gold, the stairs of silver. Precious stones studded the windowpanes. Couches covered with silks and embroidered satins were strewn with pillows of goose down. Lamps flickered in corners and tables were laid with food of all kinds – roasted meats and fragrant wines, fruits and vegetables, sweet syrups and cakes. A chill breeze blew through the palace and Hanuman shivered.

Hanuman went further into the palace and passed through the women's quarters. 'I wonder if Sita is here,' he thought. He corrected himself as he saw Ravana's women asleep, calm and contented. 'Sita could never be here. She cannot be happy and sleep dreaming sweetly while she is separated from Rama. There's no point in looking for her in the palace. I'm sure she has been imprisoned somewhere else, in an uncomfortable place with guards and spies all around her.'

Hanuman slipped out of the palace and began to explore the areas that surrounded the building. Deep in the heart of the garden which was filled with flowering trees and fragrant bushes and lotus ponds, he saw a grove of ashoka trees. 'I'm sure Sita is there,' he thought as he crept forward and, very quietly, climbed into a nearby tree, taking care not to disturb the branches and leaves. He hid himself among the foliage and leaned over.

Hanuman saw a woman, pale and sad, her hair in a single braid, her face streaked with tears. He could hear her quiet sobs as she sat there, surrounded by fearsome rakshasis, each one deformed and misshapen in some way, each one terrifying to behold. 'This gentle creature has to be Sita!' he said to himself, barely able to conceal his excitement. 'She is the most beautiful woman I have ever seen. Even though she sits here like an ordinary person, there is no doubt that she is a princess. Of course she is pining for Rama. I must tell her that he is on his way to rescue her.'

Hanuman tossed Rama's signet ring down on to the grass in front of Sita before he showed himself to her. She looked up, startled, and was even more frightened when she saw a tiny monkey approaching her. Hanuman bowed before Sita and said, 'Have no fear, my lady. My name is Hanuman and I am Rama's messenger. I am here to tell you that Rama will be here soon to rescue you. Trust me! Look, he gave me his ring to give you – so that you would know that I am truly Hanuman and not a rakshasa in disguise. I shall return to Rama and tell him that you are unharmed and waiting for him.'

'Ah,' cried Sita. 'Just hearing the word Rama makes my heart lift! Say his name again, monkey, so that I can feel happy for a few moments! Where is my beloved Rama? Is he well? Why has he not rescued me already? What is he doing?'

'Rama has made a pact of friendship with my master, Sugriva, who called together a mighty army of monkeys, hundreds and thousands of monkeys. Now that I have found you, we will attack Lanka and kill the rakshasa king who has abducted you.'

'An army of monkeys? To kill Ravana and his warriors? Surely you are joking! Has Rama lost his senses?' whispered Sita, a shadow falling across her face.

'My lady, I have just leapt hundreds of yojanas across the ocean to find you! This is not my real size. There are other monkeys like me who can change their shape and form as they please. We are all great warriors, we will succeed in our mission to destroy Ravana and Lanka. I am here as a scout to explore the city and return to Rama with details about its walls and towers, its weapons and secret passages, so that we can plan our attack. I am going to leave you now and see what I can find out about the island.'

'Stay a little longer, Hanuman! I feel Rama is close when you are here,' begged Sita, holding out her hand to the little monkey.

'I'll be back before I leave Lanka,' Hanuman reassured her. 'I must make the most of the night so that I am not noticed as I inspect the city.'

'Take this jewel from me, this pearl from the deepest depths of the ocean, that I wear in my hair. Rama will recognize it and know that you have met me and that you have my blessing in all that you do,' said Sita. 'It will remind him of his love for me and it will bring him here, swift as the wind, faster than thought itself!'

Hanuman bowed to Sita again, his palms joined in respect. He scampered up the tree and thought about what to do next. 'I can explore the city easily since I am the size of a cat. But I will have really accomplished my mission if I can take back news of Ravana himself. I should try and attract the attention of the guards so that they capture me and take me to their great king. Let me destroy this garden, they're sure to notice me if I do that!'

Hanuman slowly expanded in size. He thumped his great chest and began to tear up the ground with his strong legs, tossing mud and stones in all directions. He uprooted trees and plants and bushes and made a great noise and a commotion. 'I am Hanuman, the son of the wind god!' he roared. 'I am Rama's messenger! Beware, rakshasas! Your end is near!'

He leapt on to the ramparts of the city and knocked down a small watchtower with his fists. Rakshasa guards ran here and there, not daring to approach the giant monkey who had destroyed their king's garden and was now trying to smash the city walls. In their fear, they ran to the palace, shouting for help. They stumbled into Ravana's court and fell at his feet, panting and gasping. 'LLLLord, lord,' they stammered. 'There is a huge MMMMMmonkey in the city and he's destroying everything. He BBBroke a watchtower and he DDDDdestroyed your garden!'

Mighty Ravana turned his ten heads. His twenty eyes blazed like fire and his great voice filled the court. 'Monkey? Monkey!' he shouted. 'A monkey is destroying my city? What are you all? Donkeys? Have you been drinking? Send the kinkara army out to capture him and stop wasting my time!'

At once, the kinkaras, Ravana's elite guards, were dispatched to capture Hanuman. One hundred fighters, they were the most fearless and the most skilled in all of Lanka. But they were no match for Hanuman, who thrashed them with his tail and pummelled them with his fists and kicked them with his feet, tearing open their bellies with his sharp nails.

Ravana howled with rage when he heard about the defeat of the kinkaras and the palace walls shook. He sent his own son, Aksha, to face the monkey. Hanuman overturned Aksha's chariot and tossed the young rakshasa over the city walls on to the rocks below. Even as he defended himself against Ravana's warriors, the monkey continued to smash walls and towers and bring down tall buildings.

Ravana summoned his eldest son, Meghanada, who was known as Indrajit because he had once defeated Indra, the king of the gods, in battle. 'Go, my son!' he said. 'Avenge the death of your brother and kill that ridiculous monkey who thinks he can challenge us! I cannot think of anyone in the three worlds who can withstand your weapons and your magic!'

Indrajit rode out into the city, his chariot gleaming and his battle banner flying high. His black horses moved swiftly and chased Hanuman, who expanded still further in size and stood in the air, catching all the arrows that Indrajit attacked him with. He laughed and taunted the rakshasa warrior, leaping and jumping and avoiding all his weapons.

Indrajit realized that this was no ordinary opponent and, without hesitating any further, he released the formidable weapon of Brahma against the monkey. Hanuman fell to the ground, senseless, trapped inside invisible coils that bound him tighter than any rope. Hanuman knew what had happened and he lay still, allowing himself to be captured by the rakshasa foot soldiers. 'I must respect Brahma, the grandfather of the gods. I know this is his weapon,' he said to himself. 'My plan is working. I am sure these rakshasas will take me to Ravana. I shall not move a muscle until then.'

It took twenty-five rakshasas to carry Hanuman into the palace, where he saw the king of the rakshasas for the first time. Ravana sat upon a throne of glittering crystal whose clawed feet were made of gold. He was massive, as large and strong as a mountain peak. His ten heads wore ten crowns, each studded with bright jewels. He wore bracelets and dazzling earrings, his clothes were made of fine red silk and he looked every inch the proud and powerful monarch that he was. Ravana was surrounded by his generals and ministers who were all magnificent rakshasas, but he outshone them all. Hanuman was awestruck and in his heart he prayed for Rama's success against this formidable creature.

'Who are you? Who sent you here?' said Ravana to Hanuman, not raising his voice.

'I am Hanuman, the son of the Wind. I have come here as Rama's messenger to tell you, Ravana, that the end of the rakshasas is at hand. Your arrogance will ensure your own death and the destruction of your people. Sita, the woman you abducted out of stupidity, is no ordinary woman, and Rama, who will come to rescue her and kill you, is no ordinary man. Prepare to die, king of the rakshasas!'

'Rama? A mere mortal? Kill me? Rescue Sita? It is you who are arrogant, monkey, that you dare to speak to me like this. Kill him,' said Ravana to his servants. 'Get him out of my sight.'

'Wait, Ravana,' said a voice from the back of the court. It was Vibhishana, Ravana's younger brother, a rakshasa who believed in good thoughts and good deeds. 'You cannot kill a messenger. The rules of kingship forbid that. You can imprison him or send a message back with him, but you cannot kill him. You must abide by the rules, by the dharma of kingship, Ravana. You cannot do as you please all the time.'

'What good is a monkey in prison?' Ravana laughed. 'Fine, I won't have him killed. But I'll teach him a lesson he will never forget. No one comes to Lanka, kills my son, breaks up my city and leaves here unpunished. He's proud of his tail, like all monkeys are. Set it on fire!' commanded the rakshasa king.

The rakshasas were delighted with this idea and they wrapped Hanuman's tail in strips of cloth that were dipped in oil. They set the cloths aflame and paraded the monkey through the streets of Lanka. Hanuman was calm, wondering how it was that he felt no pain or discomfort as his tail burned like a torch made of straw.

'This is silly,' thought Hanuman. 'I can't let them lead me around like this, even though I am getting to see the city and can take note of what is where.' With an almighty burst of energy, Hanuman tore through the ropes that bound him and leapt upward, leaving his rakshasa captors in a heap on the ground. The monkey sprang from wall to wall, from tower to tower, using his great tail to set fire to everything around him. His father, the wind god, fanned the flames and soon Lanka was burning.

Their clothes and hair on fire, the rakshasas ran screaming towards the water, carrying their children in their arms as their homes crackled and burned and collapsed. There was smoke everywhere and the bright moon was dimmed as ashes and soot were carried into the air by the wind. Hanuman laughed and thumped his chest as he watched the confusion he had caused. Suddenly, he stopped. 'What have I done? I've set fire to the city, which is a good thing. But what about Sita? Will this fire spread to her grove of trees? Sugriva and Rama will never forgive me if I harm Sita. I will become famous in the three worlds as a fool!'

In his panic, Hanuman ran to the edge of the city and plunged his tail into the waves of the ocean to douse the flames. Then he rushed back to the palace garden, having reduced his size. To his great relief, he saw the grove was as green and peaceful as ever. He jumped into the clearing and appeared before Sita without fear as the rakshasis who guarded her were distracted by the fire in the city. 'You are safe, my lady,' he panted. 'How is it that this grove remains cool and green while the rest of the city burns?'

'It is the power of my faith and my love for Rama,' said Sita. 'Go, Hanuman! Bring Rama here as quickly as you can. I cannot live much longer without him.' As Sita wiped her tears, Hanuman reached the southern edge of Lanka in leaps and bounds. He expanded himself till he was as tall as the city walls and pushed back against the earth. He leapt into the air, his tail streaming behind him as he flew through the skies like a comet.

Before long, he could see the sandy beach where the other monkeys waited for him. They began to cheer and clap as they saw this marvellous creature flying through the air towards them. 'I have seen Sita!' roared Hanuman as he landed on the sand. 'Let us return to Kishkindha with the good news, my brothers. It's time to go to war with the rakshasas and bring Sita back!'

The monkeys leapt and shouted and danced for joy as they began their journey home. They sang as they went along, eating from the fruit trees and drinking from the cool waters of lakes and springs. The way home seemed so much shorter as they thought of their families with love and of the coming battle with excitement. They knew that everything now rested on their skill and their courage, and they were determined to make Rama's mission a success.

In Kishkindha, Sugriva could hear a great rumbling and he ran to Rama and said, 'The monkeys from the southern expedition are coming back. I feel sure they have found Sita and have good news for us! Come, Rama, let us prepare to welcome them.' As he was speaking, the sky darkened and the earth shook as that band of mighty monkeys approached the hilly lands of Kishkindha.

Hanuman honoured both Rama and Sugriva. Then he said, 'I have seen Sita and she is waiting for you, Rama! She sits alone under a tree, crying and pining for you. Look, she gave me the jewelled pin from her hair as a reminder for you to rescue her.'

With tears in his eyes, Rama took the jewel and pressed it to his heart. His voice shook as he said, 'We must make preparations to depart immediately. Tell me, Hanuman, did you see Ravana? What is he like?' Hanuman began to describe Ravana in all his majesty and told the gathered monkeys about Lanka and its fortifications.

Then, Rama, Sugriva, Hanuman and Lakshmana stepped away and talked quietly amongst themselves. The great monkey generals Nala and Nila, Sushena and Vegadarshi and Angada made plans for the monkey troops, dividing them into battalions and assigning them different tasks. Jambavan supervised the polishing and sharpening of Rama's and Lakshmana's flawless weapons.

In less than a day, the army of monkeys and bears was ready to march south. Hanuman carried Rama on his shoulders and Angada carried Lakshmana. Rama took charge of the troops with Sugriva and the monkey generals as his chief commanders. Rumbling and surging like the ocean itself at high tide, the army moved forward. This time, there was no singing and dancing and jumping and talking. Each monkey and each bear was focused on the task that lay ahead and marched steadily onward.

The army reached the ocean shore in what seemed like no time at all. Rama gazed over the water, as if trying to catch a glimpse of his beloved Sita on that faraway island. 'What now?' he asked Sugriva. 'How will the monkeys and bears cross the ocean?'

'Nala and Nila are the sons of Vishwakarma, the architect of the gods,' replied Sugriva. 'They will build a bridge from here to Lanka. But we need the ocean to cooperate. He must promise to keep his waves and currents under control, otherwise we will not be able to build something that holds steady.'

'No one can stop me from reaching Lanka!' said Rama, his eyes blazing. His great bow twanged and, in an instant, he unleashed a shower of arrows against the ocean that fell like rain upon the restless waters. The ocean rose up in waves that were like massive walls of water which then crashed on the shore, splintering rocks and tossing up fish and other sea creatures.

Rama continued his attack until the Lord of the Waters appeared and stood before him with his palms joined. 'Stop, Rama, please!' he said. 'Your arrows are causing great suffering to me and to all the creatures that live in the sea. We will help you build your bridge and rescue your wife. Look, I have steadied the waves and the currents. The ocean is now as calm as a lotus pond.'

Rama thanked the Lord of the Waters and put away his weapons. Sugriva summoned Nala and Nila and told them to get to work. The monkey builders drew patterns and diagrams in the sand and explained to the others what was needed. Every single monkey and bear fell to work – some uprooted trees and brought them over, others chopped branches and trimmed leaves, still others gathered rocks and stones and crushed them so that they could be mixed with sand.

Although this was hard work, the monkeys and bears made it seem

like play. Their shouts and laughter filled the air as they splashed in and out of the water, building their bridge, inch by inch, foot by foot. The Lord of the Waters kept his word – the sea was as flat as a mirror, the currents were under control and no storms gathered in the skies. Soon, the bridge was completed and the army of forest dwellers walked across it and set up camp on the southern shores of Lanka.

Meanwhile, the rakshasas continued with their daily lives and business as usual. They seemed unconcerned that an army was preparing to attack their city. One day, Ravana decided to visit Sita. Surrounded by his courtiers and several of his women, he strolled over to the grove where Sita had lived for all these months. Ravana was dressed in red as always, in fine silks which were embroidered with tiny pearls. Gold gleamed on his arms and in his ears and he wore a magnificent necklace of nine jewels.

Sita looked away when she saw him approaching her and hid her face in her hands. 'Why do you turn away from me, Sita?' asked Ravana. 'Let me see your lovely face!'

'I cannot bear to look upon such wickedness. Go away!' Sita replied.

'How can you not be interested in me? I am so much richer and stronger and more powerful than your husband. Rama wanders like a beggar in the forest with nothing to his name. He will never be a king again. Give yourself to me. Be my wife and enjoy all the pleasures of the earth,' said Ravana gently.

'I would rather spend a hundred years with Rama in the forest than a single hour with you in your palace. You have nothing to give me. Rama is coming to rescue me, you know that. Prepare yourself, Ravana, for you do not have long to live. Rama will crush you and your family and your soldiers and your people as an elephant does an ant!' said Sita, her voice rising in anger.

'You are making me angry, Sita,' snarled Ravana. 'I have been very patient with you and now I have waited long enough. You have one month to surrender to me. If you don't, I'll have you fed to these

rakshasis for breakfast. Think about it!' Ravana thundered out of the grove, with his courtiers and women following him.

At once, the hideous rakshasis who were guarding Sita crowded around her, pushing and pinching her and pulling her hair. But one of them, Trijata, said to the others, 'Leave her alone. She has enough trouble already.' The rakshasis backed away but continued to laugh and poke fun at Sita.

Ravana returned to the palace and entered the large hall where his council of ministers were waiting for him. The first person to speak was his grandfather, Malyavan, an old and wise rakshasa, who admired Ravana and had his best interests at heart. 'My son,' he said. 'Lanka is in danger. An army of monkeys and bears has landed on our southern shores. They are led by Sita's husband, Rama, and his heroic brother Lakshmana. We must prepare for war.'

'War with monkeys and humans? We are rakshasas! We fight and defeat far greater beings than this raggle-taggle lot,' shouted Ravana. 'Where are their weapons? All they have is a few miserable bows and arrows. And some rocks and stones! I will not insult my warriors by sending them out to fight forest animals!'

'Ravana, a monkey breached the city walls and set fire to your city,' said Vibhishana. 'These are not ordinary men and animals, they seem to carry the power of the gods and divine beings with them. Rama will not rest until he has rescued his wife. Give Sita back to him, Ravana. If you don't, our city and our people will be destroyed. Listen to me, Ravana. What I say is for your own good. And for the good of the rakshasa clans. Give Sita back!'

'I have no need for your advice, Vibhishana. I have ruled Lanka well without any help from you,' said Ravana, red with anger. 'Go where you will. There is no place in my kingdom for a person who criticizes me. Even if that person is my own brother. Get out of my sight!'

Vibhishana bowed to his older brother and left the hall. He walked straight out of the city and went to the southern shore of the island where the monkey army had camped. He presented himself to the sentries and said, 'I am Vibhishana, Ravana's brother. I have come to join Rama. Take me to him.'

The War

The sentries took Vibhishana to where Rama was making battle plans with Lakshmana, Hanuman, Sugriva and the other monkey generals. They had taken care to tie his hands behind his back so that he could not escape or surprise them with any unexpected movement. Since he was Ravana's brother and a rakshasa, they did not entirely trust him.

Vibhishana honoured Rama and the others and said, 'I am Vibhishana. I am Ravana's younger brother. I have come to join you against the rakshasa king.'

Hanuman and Sugriva eyed the rakshasa with suspicion. 'Why should we trust you?' asked Sugriva. 'You could be here as a spy or as a double agent. You could pretend to be our ally and send information to your brother about our plans.'

'I am not a spy. I do not approve of my brother's actions. I think he was wrong to abduct Sita. I told him he should give her back to Rama and prevent this war that will destroy the rakshasas,' replied Vibhishana calmly.

'I don't believe you,' said Hanuman. 'I think you are here because you know that after Rama kills Ravana, he will make you the king of Lanka.'

'That may be true,' said Vibhishana. 'I promise you that I will rule in his place both wisely and well. I have always been critical of Ravana and he has always disliked me. But at the moment, I can help you defeat him. You should accept me as a friend.'

'Welcome, Vibhishana,' said Rama, holding out his hand. He turned to the others and said, 'One should always accept anyone who comes in friendship. I have no doubt that Vibhishana is telling the truth and that he believes that Ravana has done many wicked things. After the war and Ravana's death, he will be a righteous king.'

Rama smiled at Vibhishana. 'Come and sit with us. Tell us all about Lanka's fortifications. Tell us about the city's defences and where the weak points are. Where should we attack? How do the brave rakshasas fight? What are their weapons? What you tell us will help us win the war more quickly.' The sentries withdrew as Rama and Lakshmana began to draw up strategies with Vibhishana and the monkey leaders.

In Lanka, Ravana's spies were able to tell him that Vibhishana had been accepted as Rama's ally. They also told him about the size of the monkey army. Ravana went to the highest ramparts of the city and looked over at the enemy encampment. It was huge and from afar he could see that the monkeys and bears were very disciplined and focused, not rowdy and chaotic, as he had expected them to be. For the first time in his life, Ravana felt the cold fingers of fear clutch his heart. But he shook himself and called for his sorcerer to appear in his court.

'Create an illusion of Rama's head,' he commanded. 'I want to take it to Sita and tell her that her husband is dead and that she should give up all hope of being rescued. Then she will surrender to me, she will have no choice.'

In a second, the sorcerer had created an illusory head, pale and lifeless with blood dripping from its neck. Ravana went quickly to the grove and called out to Sita. 'Come here, woman! Look what I have for you. There was a terrible battle last night and many rakshasas and monkeys were killed. The war is over because your weak-kneed husband is dead. I didn't have to kill him, an ordinary rakshasa was enough to cut off his head! Show her!' he said to the rakshasis.

Gleefully, one of the older rakshasis came forward, holding the illusory head by the hair. Sita screamed and fainted the moment she saw that beloved face, now so lifeless. The rakshasis revived her by splashing water on her face, but before Ravana could taunt her some more, he was called away to the war council.

Sita lay on the ground, weeping as if her heart would break. A rakshasi named Sarama slipped out of the shadows and came to her.

She wiped her tears and held her close, whispering words of comfort and solace. 'Don't cry, Sita,' she said. 'That was a magic trick, an illusion created by the king's sorcerer. Look, there is no head here. Ravana wanted to frighten you into giving yourself up to him. I know why Ravana has been called away. The generals and ministers have seen bad omens – comets falling from the sky, jackals howling and vultures circling in the skies above Lanka. Horses and elephants are weeping tears of blood and yellow-eyed women are laughing in the streets. Ravana's death is near and Rama's victory is assured.'

As Sarama was consoling Sita, a great tumult rose from the city. Horses neighed, elephants trumpeted and donkeys brayed. War drums were beaten and chariots rumbled through the streets. Rakshasa warriors poured out of their homes with their weapons ready, yelling and shouting, thumping their chests and slapping their thighs with excitement.

As the sun rose, Rama called his troops together. 'We are going into battle against thousands of mighty warriors. The rakshasas are known for their fighting skills and their courage. They are formidable opponents. But you are all brave and fearless and I know that you will fight till the bitter end. We have come this far to rescue Sita and to kill wicked Ravana. We cannot turn back and we cannot fail.'

At an auspicious moment, Rama picked up his great bow and walked to the head of his troops. Lakshmana followed behind him and after him came Vibhishana. Hundreds and thousands of monkeys and bears armed themselves with mountain peaks and rocks and stones and entire trees. They followed Rama across the flat lands to the city walls with their massive gates. The commanders went into position. Rama and Lakshmana took the northern gate which was as tall as a mountain, Hanuman guarded the western gate, Nala and Nila took over the eastern gate, and Sugriva and Angada held the southern gate.

As soon as the battle conch was blown, the monkeys and bears swarmed over the walls and gateways of Lanka, leaping over the moat with their teeth and nails bared. The rakshasas were waiting for them and set to with their clubs and maces, smashing them down in all directions. But the monkeys were swift and agile, ducking and jumping and running way from the blows. The bears were steadfast and fearless, holding their ground firmly. They hurled rocks at the rakshasas and hit them hard with the great trees they used as weapons. Soon, the ground was slick with rakshasa and monkey blood. Lifeless rakshasas lay all over the battlefield but the wounded monkeys and bears kept fighting, scratching and biting and kicking when they lost their weapons. On top of the gateways and towers, Rama and Lakshmana stood tall, releasing showers of arrows that sped through the air like lightning and found their mark, piercing the armour of the rakshasa commanders who fought ferociously on the city walls.

The monkeys and the rakshasas continued to fight even when night fell. The darkness created great confusion but the warriors fought on and on. Indrajit, Ravana's mighty son, now entered the fray. Because of a boon from Brahma, he could not be defeated in battle. His arrows flew everywhere, lighting up the darkness. He attacked Rama and

Lakshmana in particular and, in a few seconds, there was not an inch on their bodies that was not pierced by arrows. The arrows turned into writhing snakes and the brothers were bound hand and foot. Both Rama and Lakshmana collapsed, as if lifeless.

The monkeys withdrew from the battle and gathered around. Sugriva wept in sorrow and in fear, believing he had lost his friend and leader. Even Vibhishana was stunned and he knelt beside the princes, stroking their faces. Just when it seemed that all hope was lost, a storm wind arose and out of the ink-black sky came a massive bird, his wings churning the air and raising the dust of the battlefield. It was Garuda, the king of the birds. He leaned over the princes and touched them with the tips of his great wings. At once the snake arrows disappeared and Rama and Lakshmana opened their eyes, as if waking from a deep sleep. In a trice, they were back on their feet and ready to do battle again. 'Let us retire for the night,' said Vibhishana. 'The darkness will not help us and we should all get some rest.'

The next day, Ravana sent his most important generals to fight – Akampana, Dhumraksha and Prahasta. Between them, they had killed hundreds of thousands of creatures and they carried their scars from their many battles with pride. They could fight with bows and arrows, swords and spears, maces and clubs. They could ride in chariots or on horses or on elephants. Each was as large as a mountain, with arms and legs as thick and strong as tree trunks. The monkeys and bears saw them emerging from the city gates and trembled. But Hanuman, Angada and Sugriva were undaunted and they stepped out to meet the rakshasas with no fear at all.

Hanuman attacked Prahasta, knocking him off his chariot with a swipe of his tail. He leapt upon the fallen rakshasa, biting and scratching and pounding him into the ground with his fists and feet. Angada roared and smashed a great rock on Akampana's head, leaving him dead on the battlefield. Sugriva charged towards Dhumraksha, crashing into his chest with a tree trunk and knocking the breath out of him. The other rakshasas fled when they saw their leaders fall.

Ravana shook with anger when he heard that his best generals

had been killed by the monkeys. 'It is time to wake my brother Kumbhakarna. Prepare him for battle without any delay!' he roared. Teams of rakshasas scuttled towards Kumbhakarna's quarters. The giant rakshasa lay asleep, his mouth opening and closing as his snores rattled the windows and doors of his palace. Kumbhakarna was not like the other rakshasas – he had the gift of sleeping for six months at a time and it was very difficult to wake him. Because he was a giant, he ate more than all the people in the palace put together.

The royal cooks went to work, making all his favourite foods – chicken and venison and wild boar were roasted and fried, rice was cooked in milk and flavoured with almonds and raisins, mounds of vegetables were cut and mixed with fragrant spices, mountains of fruit was chopped, every sweet dish under the sun was brought to the kitchen. Barrels and barrels of wine and other choice liquors were fetched from the underground cellars. All this was piled on to carts and taken to Kumbhakarna's palace.

Meanwhile, some rakshasas jumped on his chest. Others pulled his ears and nose, still others tickled his enormous feet. Fans blew the delicious smells of food in Kumbhakarna's direction, but still the giant slept on. Finally, the rakshasas dragged kettledrums into the room and began to beat on them. A conch shell was blown into his ears and then they drove cows and sheep and other small animals over his chest. Kumbhakarna stirred. The rakshasas hurried to call Ravana so that he could talk to his brother before the giant was distracted by all the food.

'Kumbhakarna, my dear brother with the pot-ears, rise! Lanka is at war and we need your help,' shouted Ravana as Kumbhakarna rubbed his eyes and yawned, causing the rakshasas closest to him to flee for fear of being sucked into his cavernous mouth.

Kumbhakarna rolled his enormous eyes and looked at his brother. 'I'm hungry,' he said. 'I haven't eaten for six months. I feel weak.'

'Eat, eat,' said Ravana. 'We have all your favourite foods ready for you. Then gather yourself and enter the battle. The rakshasas need you, we've been attacked by an army of monkeys and bears.'

'I'd like to try monkey meat. Maybe we can eat them after I've killed them,' said Kumbhakarna.

'There'll be lots more food after the battle,' said Ravana. 'Now eat what's here and let's get going!'

Kumbhakarna ate and drank till there was not a crumb or a bone left. He stumbled out of the palace and made his way to the battlefield. The ground shook under his feet. He had no need for any weapons as he used his gargantuan hands to grab the monkeys and toss them into the sea. He trampled the bears underfoot. The rakshasa army cheered and shouted when they saw him, feeling sure that victory was close. As the giant staggered around, wreaking death and destruction, Rama and Lakshmana circled around him, firing arrows from their bows and hurling sharply pointed spears. Kumbhakarna swatted them away as if they were mosquitoes. Then Sugriva, Hanuman, Angada, Nala and Nila all joined in the attack. Hanuman hung on to Kumbhakarna's neck and bit him and punched him. Sugriva whacked his legs with trees, Angada threw stones and rocks at him, but it made no difference to the giant.

Rama realized that it was time to use the weapons that Vishwamitra had taught him about when he was a boy. 'Lakshmana!' he shouted above the din of battle. 'We must use the weapons powered by the gods! Watch me!' Rama steadied his breath and unleashed Vayu's weapon. It sped through the air with the force of a gale and chopped off one of Kumbhakarna's arms. Once more, Rama concentrated all his energies and let fly Varuna's weapon, which, too, found its mark and severed the giant's other arm. Blood poured from his wounds but Kumbhakarna lumbered on, crushing monkeys and rakshasas alike.

And then Rama used Indra's weapon, bright as lightning, powerful as a thunderbolt. It lit up the sky as it headed for Kumbhakarna. It passed through his thick neck and cut off his head with its dangling earrings. The head fell to the ground with a mighty crash. Kumbhakarna's body tumbled into the ocean and sank beneath the wall of waves that rose up to meet it. The monkeys and bears let out shouts of joy and jumped and danced around, slapping each other on the back. Ravana wept when he saw his beloved brother fall and vowed that he himself would venture on to the battlefield the next day.

The day dawned with a blood-red sky and the monkey and rakshasa warriors roared back into battle. Ravana rode out of Lanka on his magnificent chariot drawn by eight horses. He shone with his own splendour, his weapons gleaming in his twenty arms. Most of the monkeys had never seen him before and they were awestruck by his appearance. Some of them turned and fled, but Angada yelled, 'Courage, my good monkeys! Stand firm!'

That day, the sky was dark with arrows and spears and missiles, the ground was wet and heavy with bloody and broken bodies. Ravana was everywhere. His ten heads and twenty arms made it impossible to attack him from any side. Indrajit also appeared on the battlefield, sometimes visible and sometimes not as he used his magic powers to shoot arrows while standing in the sky and over the water. He was able to kill many monkeys with a single arrow and nothing the monkeys threw at him seemed to touch him. Thousands of monkeys and bears were killed that day but the army withdrew for the night with the consolation that their leaders Gavya, Gavaksha, Mainda and Dwivida had killed Ravana's younger sons.

That night, Vibhishana spoke quietly to Rama and Lakshmana. 'I know Indrajit,' he said. 'He will soon conduct a sacrifice using a black goat. He will chant spells and incantations and he will invoke the gods to make himself even more powerful than before. He will come into battle with renewed vigour and with bigger and better weapons. We must stop the sacrifice. Only then will we be able to defeat him.'

'Lakshmana will stop him,' said Rama coolly, looking at his heroic brother who knew no fear. 'Tell him where Indrajit is performing the sacrifice. Hanuman will take Lakshmana there and together they will make sure that it remains incomplete.'

Vibhishana explained the ins and outs of the palace and told Hanuman where the secret chambers lay. He also told him where Indrajit had his sacrificial pit in a hidden part of his quarters. Hanuman and Lakshmana set off, each with full faith in the other. They crept into the city and then slipped into Indrajit's palace. Following Vibhishana's instructions, they reached the sacrificial area and hid themselves in the shadows.

They saw the great rakshasa warriors who had surrounded

Indrajit waiting for him to complete the ritual that would make it impossible for anyone, god or human, to kill him. 'Loose your arrows now, Lakshmana,' whispered Hanuman. 'Attack the rakshasas so that Indrajit will be distracted.' Lakshmana raised his mighty bow and let loose showers of arrows that fell like rain on the rakshasas. Hanuman pelted them with rocks and stones. The rakshasas cried and shouted and charged towards the monkey and the prince.

Indrajit heard the commotion and looked up from his sacrifice. He saw his special forces under attack and moved to join them. At that moment, Hanuman jumped down and set free the black goat that had been tethered to the sacrificial post. He kicked away the ritual materials and destroyed the sacrifice. Dark as a rain cloud for which he had been named, Indrajit roared in anger and turned towards Lakshmana.

'Come, Indrajit!' shouted Lakshmana. 'Look at me! I am your death!'

Lakshmana and Indrajit fought for hours that seemed like days. Never had so many arrows filled the skies, never had so many spears been thrown, never had so many weapons been used with such ferocity. The two heroic warriors were equally matched, neither getting the better of the other. The rakshasas watched in amazement and even Hanuman stopped and stared in wonder. The gods and other divine beings gathered in the skies and looked down on a battle unlike any they had seen before. Indrajit and Lakshmana were now using all the celestial weapons they had at their command but they clashed in the air and neutralized each other.

Finally, Lakshmana pulled out a special arrow from his quiver. Its shaft was perfectly rounded, its feathers had come from Garuda, its golden tip was sharpened to a fine point. Lakshmana steadied his mind and said, 'If Rama is indeed the most righteous man in the world, if he is acting for the benefit of all the three worlds, then let this precious arrow kill Ravana's son!'

It was as if the gods had heard Lakshmana's prayer and placed their combined energies behind that arrow which blazed through the air like a sacred fire. Indrajit saw it coming but he could do nothing to stop it. It sliced off his head and returned to Lakshmana's quiver.

As Indrajit fell, the darkness lifted and the earth seemed to breathe deeply. In the palace, Ravana cried hot tears of grief for his son and lost consciousness.

When he revived, he wept some more. 'My son, my dearest son, best of all warriors, sweet child that played in my lap. Our palace will be dark without you, you had the capacity to challenge even the gods. I loved your brothers, too, but you were my great hope. You would have carried the rakshasas to greater glory. I wish I had not lived to see this day!'

The king of the rakshasas wiped his eyes and looked around at his dejected ministers and courtiers. 'The death of Meghanada, my son who was known as Indrajit because he defeated the king of the gods, shall not be in vain. His courage and his skills will inspire us. We shall avenge his death. Tomorrow, I myself will kill those puny humans, those princes without a kingdom, those leaders of an army of monkeys and bears. Tomorrow we shall fight for our race, for the survival of our people, for our pride and our dignity!'

But in the city, there was neither happiness nor hope. Too many rakshasas had been killed, too many families had lost fathers and sons and brothers. Rakshasa women wept and the men said to each other, 'This war will destroy us. Our king has become arrogant. He should return Sita and save us all from death and destruction.'

Still, when the sun rose, the loyal rakshasa warriors strapped on their weapons and set forth to fight once more.

Ravana rode out again in his eight-horsed chariot, looking as terrifying as the god of death himself. He was accompanied by his special guards, Mahodara, Mahaparshva and Virupaksha, who were eager to fight. Vultures and crows called out in harsh voices. Ravana's horses stumbled and dark clouds rained down dirty water, but Ravana ignored these omens of defeat. He roared like thunder as he entered the field of battle. 'Face me, Rama! Bring your brother out, too. I will kill him first because he killed my son!'

The monkey and bears and rakshasas attacked each other with renewed vigour. The great monkey warriors all moved towards Ravana and his guards, following Rama and Lakshmana and aiding their efforts. Sugriva picked up a huge tree and smashed Mahodara's elephant on the head and Hanuman went after Ravana's horses as the princes unleashed all their weapons against Ravana. Arrows filled the air as Rama and Ravana used all their magical weapons against each other.

Chariots crashed to the ground, horses and elephants were slashed and ripped apart, rakshasa and monkey alike were stabbed and clubbed and pierced. Rama pulled out his arrows that had been blessed by Brahma, Ravana countered them with arrows he had received from Shiva. The duel between Rama and Ravana went on but because of his many arms and many heads, Ravana could also counter the attacks from Lakshmana.

Ravana picked out a magnificent spear that had been made for him by Maya, the sorcerer of the gods. He whispered a mantra over it and hurled it at Lakshmana. It pierced Lakshmana in the chest and came out through his back. Lakshmana collapsed and Ravana's laughter rang through the heavens. 'Ha ha ha ha ha!' He shouted, 'I will give you time to mourn the death of my son's killer!' and went back into his city.

Rama fell to his feet beside his brother. 'O Lakshmana, how can you leave me alone in this world! First my kingdom, then Sita, now you. This is the hardest loss to bear, how will I live without you,' he wept. The monkeys and bears gathered around, their eyes streaming with tears. Sugriva summoned Sushena, the physician of the bears, and begged him to help but Sushena shook his head sadly and looked at the ground.

Suddenly, a quivering old voice spoke up. 'Hanuman, where is Hanuman?' it said. Sugriva turned to see Jambavan trying to get his attention. 'What do you want with Hanuman at a time like this?' said Sugriva fiercely, barely able to control his emotions. But Hanuman came forward and bowed before Jambavan. 'Command me, sir,' he said.

'There is one herb that can save Lakshmana's life but it grows on a mountain far away from here, across the seas and beyond the mountains where the sun rises. You will have to fetch it, Hanuman, before the first light of day touches Lanka's high towers. Listen, and I will tell you where to find it and what it looks like.' Hanuman bent over so that he could hear what the old bear was saying. 'Bring back the sanjeevani, Hanuman, you are our only hope,' whispered the bear.

Even before he had finished speaking, Hanuman had expanded to his huge size and was preparing to leap into the sky. He flew at a great pace, keeping his eyes on the horizon, looking for the mountains of the rising sun. He flew past them and landed on the peak that Jambavan had told him about. But try as he might, he could not find the sanjeevani herb. As he searched, the pale gold rays of the sun appeared in the eastern sky.

Hanuman knew he was running out of time. 'I'll just take the whole mountain with me,' he thought, and broke off its peak as easily as if he were snapping a twig. He placed the mountain in the palm of his hand and, with his tail unfurled behind him like a banner, he began his journey back to Lanka. Faster than the wind, swifter than thought, Hanuman reached the island where the monkeys and bears waited for him. He set the mountain peak down on the shores of Lanka and, in a flash, Sushena had found the herb and crushed it with oils and other plants according to Jambavan's instructions. He applied the mixture to Lakshmana's forehead and under his eyes and around his nose. Lakshmana's pale face flushed, his eyelids fluttered and he began to breathe.

'Look, Rama,' said the bear gently. 'Your brother is alive!'

Rama embraced Lakshmana and stroked his hair and kissed his face. Hanuman brought water and soon Lakshmana had recovered consciousness.

'I have had enough of this war,' said Rama with quiet determination. 'Tomorrow, I will kill Ravana and get my wife back.'

The next day, Rama fought in a chariot. Indra, the king of the gods, sent his own charioteer, Matali, to drive Rama into battle. Matali steered and manoeuvred the chariot to Rama's advantage and Rama was able to attack Ravana from all sides. The gods and heavenly sages and divine beings gathered in the sky to watch this great battle as the two opponents attacked each other with weapons that had never been seen before.

Some of the weapons bounced off each other in the air, others fell harmlessly into the sea, others failed to hit their mark, so great were the counter-attacking skills of the two warriors. The sky grew dark, the wind howled as they fought on, neither gaining the upper hand. Rama called upon all the weapons that Vishwamitra had taught him to summon, but the rakshasa king had their equal. If Ravana used arrows that turned into snakes, Rama used the weapon of Garuda, the king of the birds. If Rama used the weapons of Varuna, Ravana's shining spears cut through their nooses.

Slowly, signs of defeat began to appear – Ravana's flagstaff that carried his battle banner was sliced in half by Rama, fiery comets whizzed close to the earth, the sea churned and the tides rose, vultures and birds of prey wheeled in the air. Everyone who was watching the battle knew that these omens were for Ravana.

'Use Brahma's arrow!' shouted Matali to Rama. 'The time is now!'

Rama pulled the splendid arrow out of his quiver. It had been given to him long ago by the sage Agastya who had told him that he could use it only once and only for a great enemy. The incomparable arrow held the wind in its feathers, the sun and the moon in its shining tip, the earth in its shaft and the power of the doomsday fire in its flight.

Rama pulled his bow back to its fullest extent and concentrated on the mantras that fuelled the arrow. He held his breath and released the arrow, knowing that it carried Ravana's death with it. The arrow thundered through the air and all living beings in the three worlds shuddered at its sound. Cleaving the air, the arrow thudded into Ravana's chest and stabbed his heart. With a great cry, the mighty king of the rakshasas fell to the ground, his ten heads humbled.

A rain of flowers fell from the heavens as the celestial beings rejoiced at Ravana's death. The remaining rakshasas ran back to their city while the monkeys and bears leapt and clapped and shouted and sang. Ravana's wives came pouring out of the palace and Mandodari, his chief queen, flung herself on to Ravana's broken body and wept.

'Let us anoint Vibhishana king of Lanka with water from the ocean in the presence of his people,' said Rama wearily to Sugriva. 'And then, let Ravana have a royal funeral.'

King Rama

After Vibhishana's coronation and Ravana's funeral, Rama's thoughts turned to Sita. He called Vibhishana and said, 'Bring Sita here.' Vibhishana was surprised that Rama wanted him to bring Sita into such a public place, but he obeyed him and went to fetch Sita from the grove.

Anxious to see her beloved husband whom she had thought of night and day, Sita did not stop to wonder why Rama had not come to see her himself. Without changing her clothes or adorning herself as a princess should, she followed Vibhishana to the battlefield. Rama was waiting there, surrounded by his allies and friends.

Sita gazed at Rama, her eyes filled with love, but Rama had hardened his heart. He said to her, 'I have killed Ravana, I have won this war that was fought to get you back with the help of my friends. I have restored my reputation and the glory of my family. You were abducted by a rakshasa and lived in his kingdom without me. You are a beautiful woman – Ravana must have touched you while you were his prisoner. I cannot take you back. You are free to go wherever you want, Sita!'

Tears filled Sita's eyes, but she spoke with quiet anger to Rama. 'How can you talk to me like this? You forget that I am the daughter of Janaka, that I was born from the Earth. You speak to me as a low and common man would speak to his woman. It is not my fault that I was abducted. I have thought of nothing but you for all the time that we have been apart. My heart has always been with you. How little you know me, Rama, even after all these years.'

Sita lifted her head with pride and said, 'Build a fire for me, Lakshmana. My husband insults me in front of all these people. There is nothing left for me to do but walk into the fire!'

Rama turned away from the pain and anger in his brother's eyes. Lakshmana built a fire for Sita, who bowed to the gods and said, 'I have never thought of anyone but Rama. If I am speaking the truth let Fire, the eternal witness, protect me.' With her mind calm and her spirit serene, Sita stepped into the flames. Even as the monkeys and bears began to wail, the gods – Brahma and Shiva and Indra and Varuna and all the others – came down from the sky in their bright chariots and surrounded the fire.

Rama bowed to all the gods and stood before them with his palms joined. Brahma said to him, 'You are the greatest of all the gods, Rama! How could you let Sita walk into the fire like that? You are the creator of the worlds, you are the sun and the moon, you are Time and everything else! How could you humiliate Sita as if you were an ordinary man?'

'I know myself only as Rama, the son of Dasharatha,' stammered Rama. 'Tell me who I am. Why am I here? What is my purpose?'

Brahma spoke again, more gently. 'You are Vishnu, you are Narayana, the holder of the conch, the wielder of the discus. You

are never born and you never die, you are the three worlds, you are the universe. You contain the sun and the moon, the wind and the rain, the oceans, the earth and the sky. Wise men search for you but you are beyond understanding. Everything is in you and you are in everything. You are the best of us all, Vishnu. The gods begged you to protect the worlds from Ravana and so you took the form of a man and were born as Dasharatha's son. These marvellous monkeys who fought by your side are the sons of the gods and other celestial beings – Sugriva is the son of Surya, the sun god, and Hanuman is the son of Vayu, the wind god. The gods have been with you all this time. Now your work here is done. You can return to heaven whenever you like.'

'But what does that mean?' thought Rama, bewildered. 'Am I god? Or am I a man? How do I act in the world? Do other people see me as god? Am I always right or do I make mistakes, like other humans? How do I live the rest of my life now that I know that I am god?'

At that moment, Agni, the god of fire, rose up from the flames, carrying Sita in his arms. Her skin glowed golden, she was dressed in fine ornaments and silks that shone with the burnished hues of flames. 'Here is your wife, Rama!' said Agni. 'She has always been faithful to you. She held you in her heart and she remained pure and chaste. Take her back and honour her as she deserves.'

Rama took Sita's hand and said to all the gods, 'I always knew that Sita, daughter of Janaka, had been true. I never doubted her heart for a single moment. But she had to be proved innocent for the world to see – so that there will never be any suspicions about her character and her behaviour. She has always loved me and I have always loved her. She is as much a part of me as the rays of light are part of the sun!'

The monkeys and bears and rakshasas cheered as Rama accepted Sita. The gods smiled and then Rama said, 'If you are pleased with me, then I ask you for one more thing. Let all the brave monkeys and bears who died during this terrible war be brought back to life.' At once, the dead forest dwellers were revived, their wounds healed and their bodies made whole. They were reunited with their brothers and friends.

Shiva came forward and said to Rama, 'It is time for you to return to Ayodhya. Fourteen years have passed, your exile is over. Reclaim your kingdom from noble Bharata and rule Ayodhya wisely and well. Show the world what it means to be king, Rama. Establish dharma on earth before you come back to your true form in heaven. It is part of your purpose – to ensure that humans know the difference between right and wrong.'

'It shall be as you say,' said Rama, bowing low with his palms joined. The gods showered blessings in the form of flowers on all those who were present and went back to their homes, well satisfied with the way things had turned out.

'I thank every one of you for all your help and support. Victory in this war and the defeat of Ravana could not have been accomplished without you. It is time now for me to go home, to my beloved city and my kingdom, to my mothers and my brothers and to my people,' said Rama. 'The monkeys and bears must also return to their homes and their families. Vibhishana, prepare for our return. I leave Lanka in your safe hands. I know that with you as their king the rakshasas will never torment the three worlds again.'

'Ah Rama!' Vibhishana sighed. 'I wish to be with you when you are crowned king of Kosala. I wish to see your beautiful city and share your joy. Please let me come with you!'

Sugriva and Hanuman joined their palms before Rama and said, 'We too would like to see Ayodhya and meet your people. Take us with you, dear Rama!'

Rama smiled and embraced each of them. 'Come, my loyal allies. You are as dear to me as my beloved Lakshmana. Come and celebrate with me as I am crowned king.'

Vibhishana clapped his hands and summoned Pushpaka, Ravana's magic chariot. It was made of gold and it had comfortable seats. It flew through the air of its own accord and carried its passengers wherever they wanted to go. 'This splendid flying chariot is yours, Rama!' said Vibhishana. 'It will take us all to Ayodhya. After that, it will come to you whenever you think of it and take you where you wish.'

Amidst great rejoicing, Rama, Sita and Lakshmana climbed into Pushpaka along with their friends and allies. 'Hanuman, go ahead of us and tell Bharata all that has happened. Tell him we are on our way home!' said Rama.

The great monkey rose into the air, waving farewell with his tail as he sped onward to Ayodhya with the good news. He flew over mountains and forests and rivers and soon, in the distance, he saw Bharata's encampment outside the city. He landed gently, next to Bharata. He noticed that Bharata sat not on the throne, but on the ground. 'I am Hanuman,' said the monkey. 'I am Rama's messenger and I am here to tell you that he has killed Ravana and won Sita back. Let me tell you everything that happened in these fourteen years since he left the city!'

Tears of joy flowed from Bharata's eyes as he embraced the monkey. 'Tell me, tell me everything that my dear brother experienced in his exile. But let me first give orders for his coronation – the priests must be summoned, the sacred materials must be gathered. Those are his sandals on the throne, I have ruled only in his name. I cannot wait to return the kingdom to him.'

After making sure that his people were preparing for the ceremony and that the queens of Ayodhya had been alerted, Bharata led Hanuman to the shade of a tree and listened eagerly as

Hanuman recounted his own adventures and those of Rama, Sita and Lakshmana.

Meanwhile, Pushpaka flew through the skies and Rama pointed out all the places they had travelled over to Sita. She listened to his stories about the bridge the monkeys had built, where they had lived in Kishkindha, the place where noble Jatayu had been killed. Sita covered her face when they passed over the Dandaka forest from where she had been abducted, but she smiled at the memories of their pleasant days in Chitrakuta. Before long, they could see the river Sarayu in the distance and they knew they would be in Ayodhya within a short time.

Joyful citizens had gathered to welcome their beloved Rama. But the first thing Rama did, along with Sita and Lakshmana, was to honour his mothers, all three of them. Then he held his brothers close, his silence saying more about his happiness at their reunion than his words ever could have. Soon, the royal priest Vasishtha arrived with the other brahmins and they led Rama over to the enclosure where he would be crowned. In the presence of kings and other leaders,

Rama was anointed with water from the sacred rivers and, amidst the chanting of prayers and blessings, he became the ruler of the kingdom of Kosala. The celebration was accompanied by the giving of gifts – land and cows and money and food. The city hummed with joy for days and even the humblest of homes overflowed with abundance.

The monkeys and Rama's other allies stayed on after the coronation, enjoying Ayodhya's many pleasures and basking in Rama's company. When it was finally time for them to go, Rama showered them with jewels and other gifts. Sita placed her necklace of pearls around Hanuman's broad shoulders and the monkey shone like the moon surrounded by a garland of clouds. Hanuman wept when he had to leave Rama's side but the king embraced him and said, 'Dear Hanuman! You shall live for as long as my story is told in the world of men! In the story, you shall always be by my side, my faithful companion and the most magnificent of all monkeys. There shall never be another like you!'

Rama's forest allies departed as did the great kings and mighty rakshasas who had come to attend the coronation. The magical

Pushpaka rose into the air and disappeared beyond the clouds, promising to return whenever Rama thought of him.

Rama settled down to rule his kingdom as his ancestors had done before him. There was no sickness or hunger, people performed their duties and lived comfortably into old age. The fields and farms provided abundant grain and the markets were full of goods to buy and sell. City and country dwellers prospered together and there had never been a happier time. Rama kept track of his people's joys and sorrows and responded to their needs quickly and efficiently. But there was even more joy ahead as Sita was soon pregnant and everyone in the kingdom waited impatiently for an heir to Ayodhya's royal lineage.

One day, in his splendid court, Rama asked his ministers and informers, 'Tell me, what are my people saying? Are they unhappy? Is there anything more I can do for them?' The ministers smiled and shook their heads, reassuring Rama that all was well.

But one of his informers raised his hand and asked permission to speak. 'Lord, I have something to tell you, but I cannot say it here in the court,' he said, his eyes on the ground.

'Speak freely, my man,' said Rama. 'There is nothing that a king should hide from his advisers.'

Without raising his head, the man said, 'Forgive me for what I have to say, but the townspeople are gossiping. They say that they do not understand how you took Sita back when she had stayed so long in the house of another man.'

Rama's brow darkened and he dismissed the court, asking only his brothers to stay behind. They waited and watched as Rama seemed to struggle with his emotions. Finally, he sighed heavily and said, 'I must banish Sita from the city. The people must respect their queen, she cannot be the subject of their suspicions. Tomorrow, Lakshmana, tell Sita you are taking her to visit the wives of the sages in the forest. She has missed them and will be pleased to see those gracious women again. Leave her in the forest, near the hermitage of the sage Valmiki. He was a friend of our father's and he will take care of her.'

Lakshmana stared at Rama, horrified at what he had just been asked to do. He shook his head and started to speak but Rama silenced him. 'I have made up my mind. Please do not make this any harder than it already is.' He turned on his heel and walked away, alone, to his private chambers.

The next day, Sita was full of excitement as she climbed into Lakshmana's chariot. 'Look, Lakshmana,' she said with a smile. 'I'm taking fine clothes and perfumes for the women and sweets from the city for everyone else. They were so kind to me when I was there!' Lakshmana bit his lip and said nothing as he helped her mount the chariot.

Swiftly, they rode out of the city. Lakshmana remained silent and grim. 'What's the matter with you today?' asked Sita. 'There's a dark cloud hanging over you. Are you missing Rama? You'll be back with him soon enough. Enjoy the weather – it's lovely to be away from the city and under the open skies. Let's stop when we get to the river. We can refresh ourselves there.'

Lakshmana rode on. He stared at the road, blinking away his tears. When they got to the river, Sita dismounted and went to the edge of the water and stepped in to wash her face. As she bent over to drink from her cupped hands, Lakshmana turned the chariot around and sped away, leaving Rama's wife alone. Sita called out after him, 'Where are you going, Lakshmana? We have further to go before we reach the sages' homes!'

Sita watched in horror as the chariot disappeared into the distance. It was a while before she realized that she had been abandoned in the forest. She collapsed, weeping, on the ground, unable to think of what to do or where to go. 'How did this happen?' she wondered aloud. 'What did I do to deserve this? This must be what Rama wanted as no one would dare to do this to me without his consent! O what shall I do? Where shall I go?' she sobbed.

Sita had not noticed, but there was a group of children playing nearby. They were from Valmiki's hermitage and they ran back to tell the sage that a lone woman was weeping by the river. The sun was beginning to set. Valmiki hurried to the riverbank and saw Sita. With the power of his austerities and his divine eye, he knew immediately who she was and what had happened to her. 'I am Valmiki,' he said gently as he approached her. 'I was a friend of King Dasharatha and I know that you are the wife of his son, Rama. Come with me, the women in my hermitage will take care of you. Make your home with us.' Sita gratefully accepted the hand that he held out to her and followed the old man to his settlement.

Sita stayed in the forest hermitage, surrounded by the love and kindness of the sage's people. In a few months, she gave birth to twin boys. Valmiki blessed them and named them Lava and Kusha. He promised to care for them and to teach them, to treat them as he did his other students who lived in the hermitage. The boys grew and brought their mother much happiness, but there was a sadness in Sita's heart that she could not share with her sons. She never told them who their father was.

Though the boys looked like princes, they lived like forest dwellers, wearing simple clothes and eating roots and fruits. From Valmiki, Lava and Kusha learned the sacred texts. The sage noticed that they had sweet singing voices and so he would often teach them songs and poems that he had composed.

One day, the sage saw a hunter shoot one of a pair of birds. The female bird cried out in grief as she saw her mate fall dead to the ground. Valmiki was moved by the bird's pain and as he cursed the hunter he realized that he had spoken in a new poetic metre. When he reached his hermitage, he sent for Lava and Kusha. 'Come,' he said. 'Sit by me. I have just created a new metre and I want you to learn the poem that I will compose in it. It shall be a poem like none other. And you are the ones who shall take it into the world!' The boys brought their simple musical instruments and listened carefully as Valmiki began to recite the new poem.

Meanwhile, in the city of Ayodhya, Rama continued to rule as before. Months and years went by. Sometimes, a shadow would fall across Rama's face and his eyes would dim with unshed tears, but no one knew what was in his heart. He never mentioned Sita's name or let anyone talk about her in his presence.

One day, the royal priest came to him and said, 'Rama, you have made your kingdom prosperous and powerful. It is time now for you to perform the sacrifice of the monarchs. A king of your stature and reputation needs to show the world that he has no rivals. Let us invite all the reigning kings from around the world and the great sages as well.' Rama agreed, even though his heart was heavy as he knew that for the sacrifice to be complete he would need his queen by his side.

Invitations were sent far and wide and the city was soon filled with people from different lands. Along with kings and sages came dancers and singers and actors and acrobats and jugglers and soldiers and traders and farmers and priests – everyone wanted to be present at a sacrifice which would go on for weeks and would involve gifts of clothes and money and food from the king. Even the monkeys and bears and rakshasas who had fought so valiantly with Rama came back to enjoy the celebrations.

As the sacrifice went on, the sage Valmiki arrived there with his companions and students and settled down in the enclosure for sages. Lava and Kusha had come with him and Valmiki instructed the boys to recite the new poem wherever they could. The boys sang their teacher's beautiful poem here and there among the people and before long everyone was talking about them.

The boys soon found themselves performing for the king. Rama listened, entranced, as the boys sang the story of a great royal lineage, its joy and sorrows, its triumphs and tragedies. One day, he asked the boys, 'Whose story is this? Who are you and where did you learn this poem? Who is your teacher?'

The boys bowed before the king and said, 'This is your story, Rama. We are students of the sage Valmiki and he has brought us to this sacrifice.'

Rama listened with great attention and called his brothers and ministers as well as his allies and friends to listen with him. As the poem went on, Rama and the others who were listening learned that the boys who stood before them were the sons of Sita, born in the sage Valmiki's hermitage. Rama's heart beat faster and he quickly said, 'Go to your teacher and say to him, "If Sita is innocent, let her come here and prove herself in front of this great assembly!"'

The boys carried the message back to the sage. Valmiki arranged for Sita to be brought to the city and the next day he led her into the sacrificial enclosure.

Sita kept her eyes on the ground as she walked past the kings of the world and the assembled sages. A silence fell as Valmiki's voice rang out. 'This is the woman you abandoned in the forest, Rama. You feared the gossip of your people, but your wife has always been innocent. These beautiful boys are your sons, Rama! I brought them up in my forest hermitage for you and taught them the story of their royal ancestors. Accept Sita as the virtuous woman that she is and claim your sons for Ayodhya!'

Rama joined his palms and bowed to the sage. 'I have never doubted Sita and I know these boys are my sons. I had to abandon her to please my people. Let her prove her innocence once more, here, before the citizens of Ayodhya and the kings of the world and the great sages. Then they will all believe in her virtue.'

Knowing that something stupendous was about to happen, the gods came down from the heavens. Vayu released a gentle breeze that was laden with perfume as Sita stepped forward in her ascetic robes. 'If I am innocent, let the goddess accept me into the earth!' she whispered. The ground in front of Sita's feet opened up and a glittering throne appeared, borne on the jewelled hoods of two magnificent nagas. Heavenly music filled the air as Sita mounted the throne. The nagas slipped back into the earth, taking Sita with them.

A great silence fell. No one moved, not a blade of grass stirred, not a leaf drifted to the ground. It was as if time itself had stopped. No one knew how long this lasted, but when they returned to their senses, they all knew that Sita had gone forever. Rama, too, awoke as if from a trance. He was distraught when he realized that his beloved wife had left him. His brothers tried to comfort him but Rama was beyond solace. He embraced his sons and with his arms around their shoulders he led them away from the sacrifice. Rama gave instructions for a statue of Sita to be made from the purest, finest, beaten gold. From that day onward, the statue of his beloved queen was placed next to him at all formal ceremonies and rituals.

After Sita's departure, King Rama continued to discharge his duties as before. Rama was surrounded by his advisers, great sages who were experts in dharma and led the king through his duties. His sons were trained in the arts of kingship, learning from their uncles and their ministers how to use weapons and how to manage political and social matters.

Rama settled his brothers and their sons in neighbouring lands but he kept his beloved Lakshmana close by his side. They never spoke of Sita, but Lakshmana knew that Rama had changed, that he was no longer the man he had been in the forest.

Rama could not get used to life without Sita. His loneliness increased with the years and even though his sons made him happy his smile never reached his eyes. Although he performed all his royal duties wisely and well, everyone knew that he nursed a broken heart.

One day, a messenger arrived and asked to see Rama. 'I have something to tell you. But we must not be interrupted when we are together. No one must hear us or see us. If anyone interrupts us, even with a good reason, they will die.' Rama called Lakshmana and asked him to guard the door while he spoke to the stranger.

When they were alone, the messenger said, 'I have come from Brahma, Rama. Your time on earth is done. Return to heaven now and be united with the divine Vishnu again.'

'I have been thinking the same thing,' replied Rama. 'I have done all I can for Ayodhya and I have fulfilled my duties as a father and as a king. Yes, it is time for me to return to the gods. I shall see my beloved Sita again in heaven.'

Meanwhile, the sage Durvasa came to Ayodhya and marched straight to the palace. No one dared stop him because he was known for his temper and the terrible curses that he unleashed, even on innocent people. He said to Lakshmana, 'Open the door. I want to see Rama. I am hungry and I need a meal.' Lakshmana replied that Rama could not be disturbed. 'All right,' said the sage. 'If you do not let me in, I shall curse you and your family and this kingdom and this entire land. It's your choice.' Without hesitating for even a moment, Lakshmana entered the room. He knew the consequences of the choice he was making but he was sure that it was better if he alone died, rather than have the sage's curse affect the entire kingdom.

Rama came out and honoured the sage and gave him a wonderful meal. The sage was satisfied and went away. And then it dawned on Rama what had happened, that it was Lakshmana who had entered the room, that it was Lakshmana who would be hit by the messenger's curse. He collapsed on his throne with his head in his hands. 'Ah

Lakshmana, my Lakshmana!' he sighed. 'Even you will leave me now! Will fate show me no mercy?'

'My brother,' said Lakshmana softly, 'this was meant to be. I, too, must return to heaven. I shall wait for you there.'

Lakshmana left the palace and walked swiftly to the banks of the Sarayu river. There he lay down and concentrated his mind. He controlled his senses and slowly he ceased to breathe. Flowers rained from heaven as noble Lakshmana's life on earth came to an end.

With even Lakshmana gone, Rama made preparations for his own departure to heaven. He sent for Bharata and Shatrughna and their sons and he summoned his allies and friends, including the monkeys and bears and the rakshasas ruled by Vibhishana. In their presence, he divided his kingdom equally among his sons and bound his allies to them by oaths of loyalty. Then, on an auspicious day, Rama woke before dawn. He bathed and dressed himself in soft white silk that gleamed like moonlight. He calmed his mind and, led by priests carrying the sacred fires, Rama walked to the river Sarayu.

The townspeople followed him with their families and children. They were weeping quietly, for they knew they would never see their beloved Rama again. The monkeys and bears and rakshasas and kings from neighbouring lands also joined the solemn procession to the banks of the river.

The sun rose and Rama's face shone golden as he walked into the cool waters of the Sarayu. The citizens of Ayodhya saw the gods standing in the sky and holding out their arms to him. Brahma's voice rang out, 'Come, Rama!' And in a dazzling flash of light, Rama went back to where he had come from. But his story remained on earth, to be told over and over again by many people and in many languages, for it is one of the greatest stories the world of humans has ever known.

Author's Note

Valmiki's Ramayana is the oldest version of Rama's story that we have. It was composed in Sanskrit about two and a half thousand years ago, perhaps put together from many other versions of the same story that people were telling. The story is so powerful and so well-loved that after Valmiki poets in almost every Indian language have told it again and again over the centuries, each of them adding and subtracting incidents and events so that it fits in with their understanding of the world and of how human beings should act in it.

Valmiki's story of Rama is my favourite and there are many reasons for that. It is a story of jealousy and betrayal, of love and honour, of courage and faith, of friendship and loyalty. It is about kings and warriors, ferocious rakshasas and flying monkeys, about fathers and sons and brothers and husbands and wives. It shows us how difficult it is to do the right thing when there are many choices before us.

Most importantly, it is here that we see Rama as a human being, just like us. He laughs, he cries, he gets angry, he is sad and even lonely. Sometimes, he acts in ways that confuse us and we ask if he was always right in what he did.

Rama's story is also the story of Hinduism. Dharma tells us what we should do but it is karma – our actions – that determines what happens to us. As Hinduism developed, Rama became a god, a part of Vishnu, sent to earth to show us how to behave, to bring our dharma and our karma together in harmony, so that the world becomes a better place for us all.

Arshia Sattar
21 August 2016
Bangalore

A Note on the Author

Arshia Sattar has a PhD in classical Indian literatures from the University of Chicago. Her translations from Sanskrit, *The Ramayana of Valmiki* and *Tales from the Kathasaritsagara*, have been published as Penguin Classics. She has also written books for children, including *The Adventures of Hanuman* and *Garuda and the Serpents*.

A Note on the Illustrator

Sonali Zohra studied fine art and photography and applies the principles of both to her work. From murals to illustration on ceramic, communication design, photography and illustration for books, whatever the medium, she tries to strike a balance between colour, form and light.

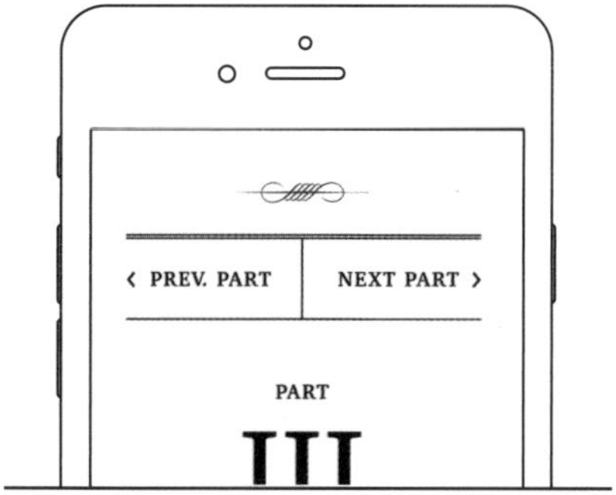

Beautiful Typography

The quality of print transferred
to your mobile. Forget ugly PDFs.

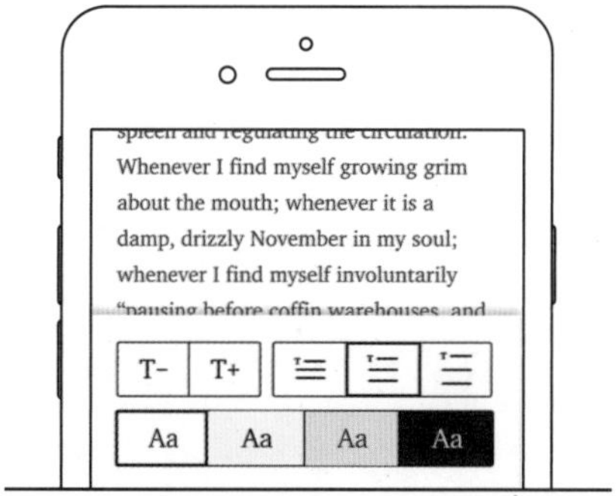

Customizable Reading

Read in the font size, spacing
and background of your liking.

AN EXTENSIVE LIBRARY

Including fresh, new, original Juggernaut books from the likes of Sunny Leone, Praveen Swami, Husain Haqqani, Umera Ahmed, Rujuta Diwekar and lots more. Plus, books from partner publishers and loads of free classics. Whichever genre you like, there's a book waiting for you.

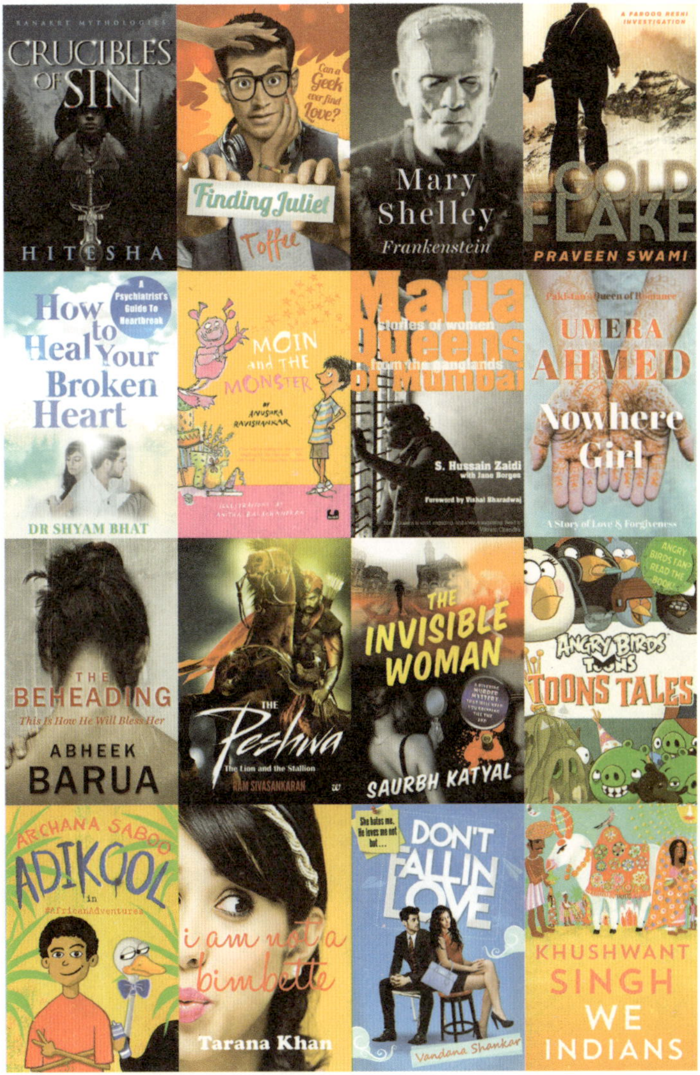
CRUCIBLES OF SIN
HITESHA
Finding Juliet
Toffee
Can a Geek ever find Love?
Mary Shelley
Frankenstein
A FAROOQ RESHI INVESTIGATION
GOLD FLAKE
PRAVEEN SWAMI
How to Heal Your Broken Heart
A Psychiatrist's Guide To Heartbreak
DR SHYAM BHAT
MOIN and THE MONSTER
ANUSHKA RAVISHANKAR
Mafia Queens of Mumbai
Stories of women from the ganglands
S. Hussain Zaidi
with Jane Borges
Foreword by Vishal Bhardwaj
Pakistan's Queen of Romance
UMERA AHMED
Nowhere Girl
A Story of Love & Forgiveness
THE BEHEADING
This Is How He Will Bless Her
ABHEEK BARUA
THE Peshwa
The Lion and the Stallion
RAM SIVASANKARAN
THE INVISIBLE WOMAN
SAURBH KATYAL
ANGRY BIRDS TOONS
TOONS TALES
ARCHANA SABOO
ADIKOOL
in
#AfricanAdventures
i am not a bimbette
Tarana Khan
She hates me. He loves me not but...
DON'T FALL IN LOVE
Vandana Shankar
KHUSHWANT SINGH
WE INDIANS

DON'T JUST READ; INTERACT

We're changing the reading experience from passive to active.

Ask authors questions

Get all your answers from the horse's mouth. Juggernaut authors actually reply to every question they can.

Rate and review

Let everyone know of your favourite reads or critique the finer points of a book – you will be heard in a community of like-minded readers.

Gift books to friends

For a book-lover, there's no nicer gift than a book personally picked. You can even do it anonymously if you like.

Enjoy new book formats

Discover serials released in parts over time, picture books including comics, and story-bundles at discounted rates. And coming soon, audiobooks.

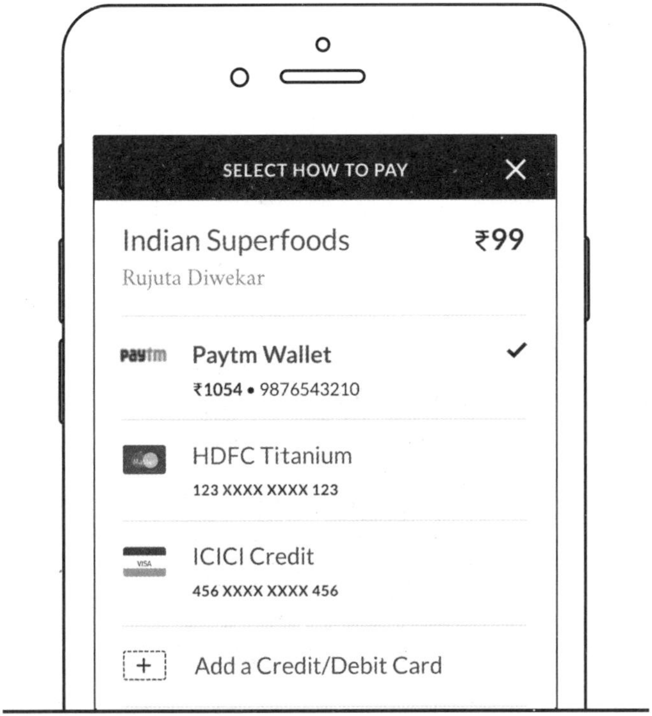

Paytm Wallet, Cards & Apple Payments

On Android, just add a Paytm Wallet once and buy any book with one tap. On iOS, pay with one tap with your iTunes-linked debit/credit card.

Click the QR Code with a QR scanner app or type the link into the Internet browser on your phone to download the app.

For our complete catalogue, visit www.juggernaut.in
To submit your book, send a synopsis and two sample chapters to books@juggernaut.in
For all other queries, write to contact@juggernaut.in